Uncovering the Mysteries of Our Past

ARCHAEOLOGY

F O R

Kids

25 Activities

Richard Panchyk

CHICAGO
REVIEW
PRESS

Library of Congress Cataloging-in-Publication Data
Panchyk, Richard.
    Archaeology for kids : uncovering the mysteries of our past : 25 activities / Richard Panchyk.
    p. cm.
Includes bibliographical references and index.
    Summary: Twenty-five activities support an overview of the science of archaeology as well as some of the secrets it has revealed from ancient civilizations throughout the world.
    ISBN 1-55652-395-5
    1. Archaeology—Juvenile literature. 2. Civilization, Ancient—Juvenile literature. 3. Antiquities—Juvenile literature. 4. Archaeology—Study and teaching—Activity programs—Juvenile literature. [1. Archaeology. 2. Civilization, Ancient. 3. Antiquities.] I. Title.
CC171 .P36 2001
930.1—dc21

                                                                    2001042134

The author and the publisher disclaim all liability for use of information contained in this book.

COVER DESIGN: *Joan Sommers Design*

INTERIOR DESIGN: *Monica Baziuk*

INTERIOR ILLUSTRATION: *B. Kulak*

FRONT COVER PHOTOS: *Machu Picchu photograph (upper left) courtesy of Donald Proulx. Jaguar drinking cup (center right) courtesy of the National Museum of the American Indian, Smithsonian Institution. All other cover images courtesy of the author.*

BACK COVER PHOTOS: *Montezuma's Palace (bottom) courtesy of Katherine Panchyk. All other images courtesy of the author.*

© 2001 by Richard Panchyk
All rights reserved
First edition
Published by Chicago Review Press, Incorporated
814 North Franklin Street
Chicago, Illinois 60610
ISBN 978-1-55652-395-3
Printed in the United States of America

FOR CAREN AND MATTHEW

Contents

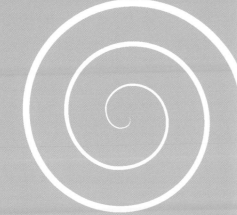

Acknowledgments

I would like to thank all those who inspired and cultivated my love of archaeology and things old, especially John Vetter, Donald Proulx, Robert Paynter, and Philip Scandura. I am grateful to the Pocumtuck Valley Memorial Association of Deerfield, Massachusetts, for allowing me to hone my teaching skills at Memorial Hall and the Indian House. Thanks to the University of Massachusetts for giving me the opportunity to teach archaeology at the college level. Additional thanks to Donald Proulx of the University of Massachusetts for his support and encouragement and for allowing the reproduction of his photographs of South America; and to John Vetter of Adelphi University for allowing me to observe and participate in the Leeds Pond excavations. Thanks to the Garvies Point Museum in Glen Cove, New York, and the National Museum of the American Indian in New York City for their support. Very heartfelt thanks to John Vetter and John Martin for taking the time to review the manuscript for accuracy. Thanks to Kathleen Freedman, Amy Newman, Katherine Panchyk, Robert Panchyk, and Caren Prommersberger for use of their terrific photographs. Thanks to Caren Prommersberger for lending her editing and indexing skills. Thanks to acquisitions editor Cynthia Sherry for her support and enthusiasm, and also to project editor Jerome Pohlen. And last but never least, thanks to Caren and Matthew for their patience, support, and understanding of the time requirements of putting together a book.

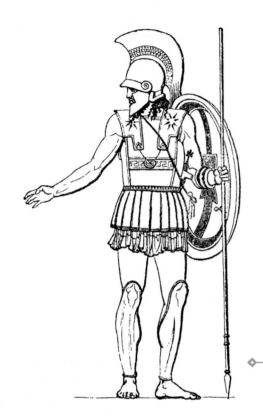

Last dinosaurs die out	65 million B.C.
First Ramapithecus	14 million B.C.
First Australopithecus	4.5 million B.C.
First Homo habilis	2.5 million B.C.
First Homo erectus	1.9 million B.C.
First Homo sapiens neanderthalensis	200,000 B.C.
First Homo B.C. sapiens A.D. sapiens	45,000 B.C.
First humans arrive in the New World	20,000–15,000 B.C.
Last Ice Age ends, Mesolithic period begins, first attempts at farming	10,000 B.C.
First Neolithic villages	6000 B.C.
Sumerian civilization at its peak	2600 B.C.
Great Pyramid of Cheops built	2550 B.C.
Shang Dynasty begins in China	1700 B.C.
Height of ancient Greek civilization	450 B.C.
Alexander the Great invades Egypt	332 B.C.
Alexander the Great invades Babylonia	330 B.C.
Height of ancient Roman civilization	100 B.C.
Julius Caesar assassinated	44 B.C.
Mount Vesuvius erupts and buries Pompeii and Herculaneum	A.D. 79
Great Wall of China originally built	220
Classic Mayan civilization begins	300
End of the Roman Empire	450
Vikings land at Newfoundland	1000
Cortés begins conquest of the Aztecs	1519
Pizarro begins conquest of the Inca	1532

Time Line

INTRODUCTION

What Is Archaeology?

Look around your room. What do you see? Chances are, you see books, magazines, toys, and clothing. These items are your *material possessions*, the things you own in life. Now make a list of everything in your room that is in plain sight. How many of these things do you think you'll still have in 20 years? What will happen to the rest of the stuff?

Most material possessions eventually end up in the trash can, and then get hauled off to a landfill many miles from where you live to slowly decay. Why? As you know, toys break, clothes become too small, and stuff that was cool when you were younger becomes very uncool. We live in a *disposable culture*, where most things are thrown away.

This disposable culture we live in is nothing new. One million years ago it was the same. Even the earliest humanlike creatures that roamed the earth had a few possessions, including tools made of rock. What do you think happened when a stone tool broke, or when a spear was thrown and lost?

Since material possessions have existed, people have been losing them, leaving them, and throwing them away. In a nutshell, archaeology is the science of finding and studying material possessions lost or discarded in the past.

Why is it a science? It certainly does not look like a science on TV and in the movies, where brave men and women with whips and knives and guns thrash their way through jungles and deserts against all odds to single-handedly find glorious ruins and treasures.

In truth, there are plenty of archaeological sites in jungles and deserts, and archaeologists sometimes do make the kind of discoveries you see on the big screen. But most of the "big" discoveries don't involve piles of gold or deadly booby traps. What archaeologists do come across in most excavations are thousands of everyday

artifacts—bits and pieces of the past—ranging in size from smaller than your pinky fingernail to twice as big as you. And, though you might not think so, every scrap of the past—no matter how small—can tell us fascinating stories about the people who made and used it.

Archaeology is the best tool we have for solving the mysteries of ancient life. In this book, you will learn about how archaeologists work and what they have discovered so far about the past, from the earliest humanlike creatures a few million years ago all the way up to about 100 years ago. You'll also have a chance to do some fun activities that will help you understand archaeology and the amazing cultures that have been uncovered underfoot.

How Archaeology Works

Howard Carter, a 49-year-old archaeologist, had been working in Egypt for years. He was certain that the tomb of King Tutankhamun lay in the bedrock under the hot sun of the Valley of Kings, where more than 30 tombs had already been found. To some people, it seemed unlikely there could be any more tombs crammed into the Valley, but Carter was insistent. He based his beliefs on the discovery of a blue-glazed cup and some jars containing linen used to wrap mummies. Both of these finds carried the royal seal of Tutankhamun.

Carter persuaded a rich Englishman, the earl of Carnarvon, to fund the excavations in Egypt one last time, as he had done for the past 15 years.

The years flew by—1918, 1919, 1920, 1921—and no significant finds were made. The digging seasons were short due to the weather conditions in Egypt, not to mention the flood of tourists that visited the already popular Valley of Kings. It was frustrating to have to wait for the months to pass until the next season. In 1922, Carter met with Carnarvon in England, and learned that Carnarvon wanted to call off the expedition and cut off the money. Without money, Carter could not pay his workers or buy the necessary supplies and food. "How can he do this to me?" Carter must have thought, but Carnarvon's doubts seemed reasonable. If the tomb had not been discovered yet, what made Carter think it would be found this time? After pleading with Lord Carnarvon, Carter finally got his wish. Work could carry on.

On November 4, 1922, workers found a staircase leading to a doorway. The doorway was only feet away from the entrance to the excavated tomb of another king, but Carter still thought this could be it. He ordered the trench filled until the patient Lord Carnarvon could make the trip from England.

On November 26, Carter and Carnarvon stood at the doorway to the antechamber. The air was thick with anticipation as Carter opened a hole into the room. When his candle brought the first light the tomb had seen in centuries, he was amazed at what he saw. He described seeing "strange animals, statues, and gold—everywhere the glint of gold."

That day was one of the most important in all of archaeological history. Though the tomb had been partially looted (things had been stolen by thieves, perhaps not long after the burial), it was mostly intact. Inside the tomb were unimaginable treasures: gilded and inlaid chairs, stools and tables, game boards, gem-encrusted jewelry, statues of gold and silver, musical instruments, solid gold daggers, works of art, and of course, the beautiful golden coffin of Tutankhamun.

◇◇◇◇◇◇◇◇◇◇◇◇◇◇◇◇◇◇◇◇◇◇◇◇◇◇

As spectacular as it was, in many ways the story of the discovery of King Tutankhamun's tomb is typical of everyday archaeology.

Most sites are not found instantly. Though people often focus on the moment of discovery, they often forget how long it takes to find the site in the first place. Archaeology is expensive, as Howard Carter knew. By 1922, Lord Carnarvon had spent what amounted to millions of dollars in modern money on Carter's digs. In real life, big announcements about spectacular archaeological finds often come after the excavations have been going on for years. Because they take so much time and money, you would think that excavations are not often done; however, modern laws often require areas be checked for possible archaeological sites before anything is built on the land. Even then, research should still take place before any real digging is done.

There are eight basic steps to archaeology. Understanding what they are will help you discover how archaeology works.

1. *What do you want to find?*

The first question an archaeologist should ask is: *What do I want to find?* Though many times strange and wonderful things are found that were not at all expected, it is better to first have a specific plan. Howard Carter wanted to find the tomb of King Tutankhamun. Along the way he found other artifacts, but he had a specific goal. The famous German archaeologist Heinrich Schliemann set out to find the mythical city of Troy, as you will see in Chapter 5. Even with prehistoric cultures, a specific goal is possible. In these cases, archaeologists may be trying to answer questions such as: *What kind of religious ceremonies did the people have?* or, *How did their diet change over time?* Whatever their goals, archaeologists still collect all the evidence they find, not just the artifacts that will help them answer their questions.

2. *Research*

Once a goal is set, it is time to hit the books. The great civilizations that began about 5,000 years ago are usually mentioned in various historical accounts. Unfortunately, by A.D. 400, the world's greatest ancient library in Alexandria, Egypt, with more than 700,000 rolls of papyrus, has been destroyed by invading armies.

Early books were handwritten and did not survive well. With the invention of the mechanical printing press in 1454 by Johannes Gutenberg, many more books could be printed than before. Now the old, handwritten texts could be mass-produced, including some of the earliest Roman and Greek legends and histories.

Have you ever played the game of Telephone? If so, you know that as time passes, information can get mixed up and details can be lost in the translation. That is why early texts are valuable resources for archaeologists. The closer in time the writer is to the event being written about, the better. In the pictures on the next page, you'll see a page from a history of England written in Latin and a page about the history of Rome written in an early form of Italian, both dating to the early days of printing. What important information do you think an archaeologist could get from these pages?

The first books to be printed on Gutenberg's press were copies of the Bible. Archaeologists have been referring to the Bible for many years, especially the parts of it that tell stories about horrific battles and invasions, large armies, great fires, mythical ancient places and monuments, and the reigns of many different kings. There is a whole division of archaeology called *Biblical archaeology* devoted to uncovering the places and events mentioned in the Bible. Some scholars even prefer to go back to earlier versions of the book, written in Hebrew and old Greek, thinking that something might have been lost in the translation to English.

The Bible is by no means the only book to refer to. Many civilizations have left behind fragments of texts and other clues. The explorers and conquerors, beginning with Alexander the Great and Marco Polo and continuing through time all the way to Lewis and Clark, also saw things on their journeys and told others or mapped them out.

The study of people who lived during times that were well documented—about whom there are many books and documents, maybe even photographs—is called *historical archaeology*. As you will see later, research is a very important part of historical archaeology.

Archaeology became a true science in the late 19th century, when people like Heinrich Schliemann carefully recorded their finds. The development of the science of *geology* (the study of rock formations over time) helped scientific archaeology become possible, as people realized the true age of the earth. Today, in the 21st century, archaeologists rely on the scientific research done by archaeologists who came before them.

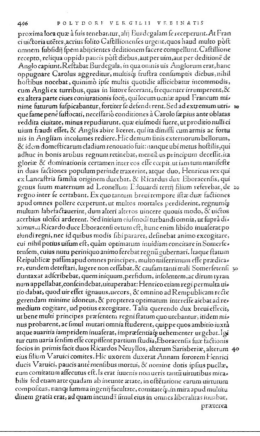

▲ *The leaf from a book on the history of England (left) dates to 1534 and the leaf from a book on ancient Rome (right) dates to 1554, not long after the printing press was invented. Archaeologists are always eager to get any information they can about the cultures they are excavating. Often, the oldest surviving records are the most accurate.*

3. Money

Without funding, there would be no archaeology. Ever since the first real archaeological excavations took place about 150 years ago, money has been an issue. As you saw before, Howard Carter's excavations used up lots of money. If he did not hire workers to dig, it would have taken him perhaps a hundred or so years to find the tomb by himself—never mind that he died at the age of 66! A modern excavation needs many workers, tools for digging, equipment to analyze the artifacts, and housing and food for the excavators. While these days college students often work at digs for free, just to get experience, excavations are still expensive. Universities and other groups sponsor research, offering what are called *grants*—money set aside for a specific research purpose. Archaeologists write grant proposals and compete for the money to fund their research. Sometimes, as in Howard Carter's case, a single individual is willing to fund work—remember in the movie *Jurassic Park*, the old bearded man named John Hammond, who owned the park and was funding the work of the paleontologists who were looking for dinosaur bones?

Funding can pay off nicely when an important site is found. Modern universities compete with each other for the prestige of conducting major excavations. The better the reputation a school has, the more students it attracts, because the students know they will have better chances of getting jobs if they graduate from a prestigious university. Of course, when more students attend, more money comes into the university.

Recently, money has become less of an issue for archaeologists. New laws make environmental and archaeological investigations a required part of many highway and building construction projects. Before anything can be built or bulldozed, archaeologists investigate the area and write a report with their findings. If they discover a valuable archaeological site, they excavate and try to save as much as they can. Funding comes from the state or sometimes the federal government. This type of archaeology is known as *cultural resource management*.

4. Survey

Once a goal is set and funding obtained, the exact site has to be selected. Survey is the best way to do this. There are different kinds of survey for different conditions. In the dry and isolated regions of Peru, for example, *surface survey* is possible because there are probably clues right on the surface of the ground. *Aerial surveys* are good for spotting patterns in rocks, or discoloration of plants due to buried walls. This cannot easily be seen from ground level. The next time you are in

▲ *The view from an airplane flying over Europe. Can you see towns? The square patches in the distance are farmland. The ideal height to see clear details is a few thousand feet above the ground.*

▲ **Surface survey in Peru.**

an airplane, look out the window and see how clearly you can spot the different features of the land below. Sometimes, an "aerial" survey can be done from a nearby hilltop.

Other kinds of survey are done below ground. Using electrical current, or detection of magnetic patterns, you can figure out if there are buried features. By running a grid of wires through a site, you can see where current flows freely and where it is disturbed by something buried in the ground. This only works for large things such as the remains of walls.

Surface survey is an easy way to see if there are any visible remains of the past lying on the ground.

MATERIALS

◆ *Yardstick or tape measure*
◆ *4 sticks or small tree branches*
◆ *4 pieces of string, each 12 feet long*
◆ *Black pencil*
◆ *Graph paper*
◆ *Box of toothpicks*
◆ *Yellow, orange, and red pencils*

Go outside and pick an item to survey. It could be rocks, flowers, bottle caps, whatever you think you'll have the best chance of finding. Now measure out a 10-foot by 10-foot square. Use four sticks to mark the corners of the square. Tie each piece of string from one corner to the next. Draw an outline around a 10-by-10 box space on your graph paper. Each square will equal one square foot. First, mark each item you find by sticking a toothpick in the ground next to it. Now measure about where each item is located in the grid. For example, if it is about 3½ feet from the left side of your grid and less than 1 foot from the bottom of the square, make a tick mark in the corresponding square on the graph paper.

When you are done, color in the squares on the graph paper according to the *density*, or how many in each square foot, of items you have found. If you found 1, color the square yellow. If there were 2–3, color it orange. If you found 4 or more in the 1-foot area, color it red. Though this is a little primitive, it shows clearly the areas that have the most "artifacts."

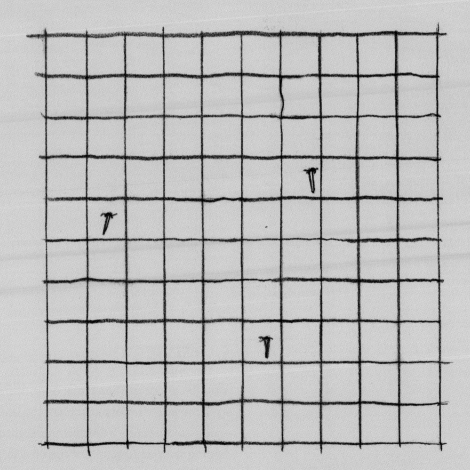

▲ **Aerial survey can be done other ways besides from an airplane. In this part of Peru, you get a very clear picture from atop a hill.**

5. Testing

A full-blown excavation is not done immediately after the survey. Even if the survey indicates a major site might lie a few feet underground, test digging is done to pinpoint the best location to excavate. The potential site is mapped out on a grid, and a few different locations are picked for the shovel tests. In a shovel test, small pits, usually less than a foot in diameter, are dug so that archaeologists can take samples at different places and map out what they have found. It is also a chance to preview the *stratigraphy*, or layering of the soil, throughout the site. This will be discussed in more detail in upcoming chapters.

Let's say you do a few shovel tests and find stone tools known as arrowheads at about 2 feet below the surface each time. You can be fairly sure the site is about that depth. It doesn't mean you can be careless when excavating, but you can certainly go faster when digging through the first 1½ feet of soil.

Finding the arrowheads at different depths in different places, say 2 feet, 3 feet, and 4 feet, could mean that either a force of nature changed the layering of the ground, that what is now flat land used to be hilly, or that human intervention has changed the location of different levels of soil. Can you think of one activity that modern humans could do to disturb a site?

Each shovelful of dirt from the test pits is sifted through a screen to let the dirt pass through, leaving only pebbles, rocks, and possible artifacts. Whatever is found is kept for reference. If the archaeologist decides not to excavate at the site for some reason, future archaeologists might be able to look through the test finds and decide if they want to work at the site.

6. Excavation

Once a site is selected, the head archaeologist looks at all the information that has been collected about the site and picks one or more 5-foot by 5-foot squares to excavate. The word *excavate* comes from the Latin word meaning "to hollow out." Entire sites are not normally excavated. First of all, most sites are very large, the size of a village or even a city. It would be too expensive and take too much time to excavate everything. For example, the famous Çatal Höyük site in Turkey was first discovered in 1958, but only about ⅓₀ of the site has been excavated! Parts of ancient Pompeii, Italy, are still being excavated, 250 years after its discovery. Besides cost and time, the most important reason of all not to dig an entire site is that once something is taken out of the ground in which it was buried, its *context* is lost forever. Context is what surrounds an object and helps to give it meaning. A crayon in its box with the other 63 crayons is in its context. By itself, it is removed from its context and you cannot get as much information about what it is and what it does. If you were an archaeologist in the year 4000, and you did not know what a crayon was, it would be easier to figure out if you saw it in its context in the box with the rest of the crayons.

When artifacts are placed in museum displays, they are often hundreds or even thousands of miles from where they were found. Though we

▲ *Excavation is usually carried out in checkerboard-like squares of uniform size.*

can learn a lot from the artifacts alone, it is important to preserve their context at part of the site. Future archaeologists may have better technology at their disposal, so they might learn even more from excavation.

When the 5-foot by 5-foot squares are selected and the digging starts, archaeologists and volunteers work long days throughout the length of the excavation season. For Howard Carter, the season was between October and December, but for most modern excavations it is during the summer, since some archaeologists are also college professors, and their students are usually the volunteers who help excavate during summer breaks.

Excavation itself is slow and requires close teamwork. A single 5-by-5 square can take more than a week, especially the deeper the site is buried. Dirt is not removed with a shovel, it is scraped away with a trowel. Every inch of dirt must be run through a screen, removing the soil and leaving twigs, rocks, and possible artifacts. Excitement buzzes around the camp when a major artifact or feature is found. The head archaeologist is called over to examine the find.

▲ *A trowel's triangular shape and flat, sharp edge make it the perfect archaeological tool.*

A screen saves an archaeologist time by filtering out all the dirt and leaving possible artifacts. ▶

The artifact is photographed and plotted on a map of the site, so that once it is taken from its context, there will be a way to figure out where it went, kind of like having a drawing of the crayon box mentioned before. Though some large artifacts may be kept in place for a while, if excavators don't remove the finds, they can't continue digging to what may be an older level hidden beneath. Plastic tarps can be used to cover and protect the site when rain arrives, but even after the rain ends, the ground still has to dry out for hours, or sometimes even days, before digging can resume. Can you imagine trying to dig in mud?

When the season is over, work stops until the next season begins. Unfortunately, sometimes damage is done to the site over the off months. Natural forces like storms and erosion can cover up parts of a site, and sometimes people come and take artifacts or vandalize sites.

7. Dating and Analysis

Though many artifacts are examined while the digging is still going on, there are usually many thousands of artifacts found at each site. The artifacts go back to the university leading the excavation, where students and archaeologists can study them during the school year to help them prepare for the next season's dig.

There are lots of things about an artifact to analyze. What is it made of? Where did that material come from? How was it made? What was its purpose? Is it rare or common? This is the time to hit the books again and see what else has been written about similar artifacts.

This is also the time to catalog each artifact. Howard Carter's finds in the royal tomb were photographed as they were found, with a small numbered piece of paper laid on top of each item. These hundreds of items were then removed from their context and studied and catalogued. Each artifact was examined carefully. Exact measurements were taken and descriptions were written.

The date of a site is often the most important single fact to emerge from the whole excavation. If Joe Smith, for example, found that the date of the site he was excavating did not match up with what the myths said about the lost city of Pacifica, it would be very important. It might mean that the legend was wrong, or perhaps the site he was excavating was not Pacifica, but some other lost city. Maybe he would become discouraged and want to try excavating somewhere else.

Dating a site, or figuring out how old it is, can be very simple or extremely complicated. Old Roman coins have pictures of emperors on the obverse (front), and all you must do is look at a reference book to match up the coin with the emperor. Later coins have actual dates on them.

Dating Coins

Coins can help archaeologists date a site.

MATERIALS
- ◆ *Handful of coins (at least 20)*
- ◆ *Pen or pencil*
- ◆ *Paper*

Take the handful of change and write down the dates of the coins on a piece of paper. What is the earliest date you have? What is the latest date? What is the average of all the dates? Use a calculator and add up all the dates, then divide by the total number of coins to find the average age of the coins. If you found these at a site, what could you say for sure about the date of the site? You will read more about this dating method in Chapter 7.

If the dates on the coins were faded, how could you tell their approximate age? Look in a coin handbook and find out when each type of coin, such as a Lincoln penny or a Jefferson nickel, was first minted.

▲ *These Roman coins were found in England and date back to the 4th century.*

It is not always exact, though, because people use coins long after they were minted (made).

Most dating is not so simple. Archaeologists try everything from careful analysis of the style of the artifact to chemical tests on the artifact to find out how old it is. Since there are so many different ways to tell how old something is, you will read about and experiment with each of these methods in detail in the other chapters of this book.

8. Preservation

Anything that has been buried in the ground is dirty, covered with soil that is sometimes caked on. Even King Tutankhamun's treasures, though not exactly buried in dirt, still needed to be cleaned after thousands of years of gathering dust.

At an ordinary site, much of the cleaning is done while the item is still being excavated. In the laboratory, small brushes and even wooden toothpicks can be used to clear dirt from tiny crevices in an artifact. If it is made of stone or another material that will not corrode, it can be soaked in water for a while to loosen up some of the hardened soil.

Once the artifact is cleaned, it can be preserved. Some materials, as you will see, are less fragile than others. Broken pots or statues can be pieced and glued back together. The archaeologist can decide if he or she wants to restore them further by filling in the missing pieces with modern clay, but sometimes rebuilding part of an artifact is the only way to preserve it. The beautiful paintings on the front of a large lyre (an instrument similar to a harp) found in Mesopotamia were in good condition, but the wood holding the lyre together had deteriorated badly. The only way to save the instrument was to reconstruct the wood parts and replace the strings. Fragile artifacts can be put on display as long as they are kept in special humidity- and temperature-controlled conditions. The most fragile artifacts (usually made of paper or cloth) must be kept in low, soft light because the harsh light of ordinary incandescent bulbs can worsen their condition.

◇◇◇◇◇◇◇◇◇◇◇◇◇◇◇◇◇◇◇◇◇◇◇◇◇

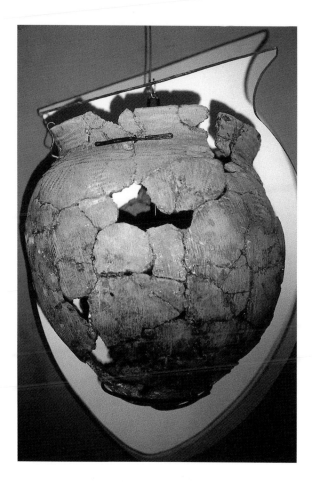

▲ **This Native American pot has been pieced together.**

This is just a brief overview of how archaeology works. You'll see these topics come up again and again throughout this book. In the following chapters, you will go on a journey through time, following the progress of our human ancestors from millions of years ago all the way up to the present. Along the way, you will perform experiments, activities, and games to help you understand what archaeology is, and how the different cultures that existed through the ages lived and died.

◇◇◇◇◇◇◇◇◇◇◇◇◇◇◇◇◇◇◇◇◇◇◇◇◇

2 The First People

Roughly two and a half million years ago, somewhere on the sunny African savannah, 63 million years after the last of the dinosaurs died, a short, hairy apelike creature standing on two legs picked up a large stone and intentionally struck it against another stone. A piece flew off, giving what was once a dull, round rock a sharp edge.

The creature realized that with a piece broken off, the stone would make a better tool, perhaps to cut a branch

Teamwork

The study of ancient plant remains is called paleobotany, *and the study of other ancient animals' remains is called* paleontology. *The study of human ancestors' bones and biology is called* biological anthropology *or* physical anthropology. *The study of the artifacts that humans and humanlike creatures, known as hominids, made is called* archaeology. *Archaeologists rarely work alone. Depending on what they find, they may bring in* paleobotanists, *physical anthropologists,* geologists *(to study rock formations),* geomorphologists *(to study soils and landform development),* chemists *(to perform tests on artifacts and the soil),* climatologists *(to figure out what weather was like thousands or even millions of years ago),* ethnographers *(to study living descendants of the people whose remains are being excavated) and other experts in related fields. They may also bring in* pilots *to fly overhead, and* photographers *to take professional pictures both in the air and from the ground. The reason so many other experts get involved is that humans do not just create artifacts—humans both change their environment and adapt to their environment in many ways, and these experts can help us understand exactly how.*

from a bush or dig up roots to eat. Imagine the sound of the fist-sized rock as it hit the second rock. While creatures like these had been using sticks and rocks as tools for thousands, maybe millions of years already, this was the first time one of them modified a rock to make it more useful. This smart creature was pleased the trick worked, and remembered it for the next time he had to cut something. He realized he could strike the rock two or three times to make even sharper edges.

The first time one rock struck another, everything changed. The creature now had an advantage over all the other creatures on the great plains of Africa. He could not only use tools, he could make tools. When he whacked that rock for the first time, another exciting thing happened. Archaeology was made possible. The creature had just created an *artifact*, an item modified and used by humans or humanlike creatures.

There were many apelike animals roaming the earth before the first tools were used. Ramapithecus existed 14 million years ago. Australopithecus, from Latin, meaning "Southern Apes," appeared almost 5 million years ago. These creatures walked upright on two legs at least some of the time, but most likely did not make tools yet. Raymond Dart made the first discovery of Australopithecus in Taung, South Africa, during the 1920s. The bones Dart found were of a five-year-old child, which he claimed was a possible ances-

tor of modern humans. Dart was ridiculed and the discovery of "Dart's Child," as it became known, was dismissed by some scientists. Similar discoveries were made in the following years, however, and scientists could no longer deny the similarities between humans and these ancient creatures.

Finally, in the Afar region of Ethiopia in the 1970s, archaeologist Donald Johanson discovered a spectacular skeleton of an Australopithecus, which he nicknamed Lucy. Though only 40 percent of its bones were found, it was the most complete Australopithecus skeleton ever found. Johanson could tell a great deal about Lucy and her species from those bones. In fact, he even wrote a whole book just about Lucy!

Meanwhile, the Leakey family was making great discoveries of Australopithecines in a part of Tanzania called the Olduvai Gorge. This gorge was created by a fault in the earth and exposed many layers of rock and earth going back 2 million years. In excavating these layers, the Leakeys exposed what they called "living floors" where they found Australopithecus bones. We have learned that these *nomadic* (this means they roamed around and slept in different places, wherever food was most available), humanlike animals were around for millions of years before another, more advanced creature appeared.

New discoveries are still being made, and the recent announcement of a new species and genus of creatures has shown that we still have much to learn about the human family tree. *Kenyanthropus platyops* dates to 3.6 million years ago and was first discovered in 1998 in Kenya by a team led by Meave Leakey. Tests have shown Kenyanthropus to be different from Australopithecus, with a much flatter face.

◇◇◇◇◇◇◇◇◇◇◇◇◇◇◇◇◇◇◇◇◇◇◇◇◇

Making Footprints

Mary Leakey made a spectacular discovery at Laetoli, Kenya. She found a set of ancient humanlike footprints in ash, preserved for millions of years because they were covered as soon as they hardened. From these australopithecine footprints, she was able to figure out roughly how tall the creatures were. How?

MATERIALS
- *Sandy beach or muddy ground*
- *Yardstick or meterstick*
- *Your height (in centimeters or inches)*
- *Calculator*
- *Paper*
- *Pen or pencil*
- *Plaster of paris (optional)*

First, take off your shoes and socks. If you are on a beach or in a sandy playground, use the yardstick to flatten out the surface by dragging it across the sand as you walk backward.

Now take a few steps, so that you are about a yard or two from the area you have cleared. If you are in a muddy place you don't have to flatten anything first. Start walking at a normal speed and step right through the flat sand or mud. Next, measure the distance of your stride in inches or centimeters, from heel of the back foot to toe of the next. You should have three or four strides' worth of measurements. Using the calculator, enter each of the measurements (they might be a little different from each other), and then divide by the number of strides to get the average stride length. Next, divide your height by the average stride length. Write down the number. Now flatten the sand again and have a friend do the same thing you did. Is their height divided by their stride about the same as yours? Obviously, this is not an exact science, but archaeologists can tell if a creature was four feet tall or six feet tall by using this method.

If you have plaster of paris handy, you can pour it carefully into a footprint. Pour it about 1 inch deep—this works best in dirt or mud, not sand. Let it set for 15 minutes, then gently remove it. Let it dry completely for 2 hours. You should have a plaster cast of your footprint!

You probably know archaeologists have to dig deep into the ground to find anything. But do you know why? Why are sites almost never found at ground level? Did ancient people purposely cover their own tracks and make it harder for us to find any trace of them?

For a good answer, we have to look to nature. Most of the time, it is nature that creates a *stratigraphy*, or layering of the earth over time.

◆ ORGANIC MATTER

Anything that is alive or was once alive is known as *organic matter*. This includes all animals and plants. If you live where there are trees, chances are you have picked up a rake at least once in your life and bagged some organic matter. It is not an easy job; the more you rake, the faster the leaves seem to fall.

Now imagine a whole forest's worth of leaves. Obviously, with nobody to rake them up, the leaves stay where they have fallen. In the spring, the trees sprout new leaves, but in the autumn the cycle begins again. What happens to all these leaves? Eventually, as all organic matter does, the leaves at the bottom of the pile begin to *decompose*, crumbling into smaller and smaller pieces.

Together with decaying wood from broken tree branches, the leaves become a rich blackish dirt called *humus*. The organic matter helps provide food for worms and nutrients for new plant life. Humus is usually the top layer of earth, just below ground level, consisting of soil mixed with organic

▲ *Leaves, twigs, tree bark, and insect and small animal remains decay and make up the rich top layer of dirt known as humus.*

matter. As the archaeologist digs deeper, the color of the dirt becomes lighter shades of brown. This means there is less organic material in the dirt and more tiny bits of rock. The lighter soil was once humus, but was eventually depleted, or drained, of its organic nutrients. The different colors of the soil help the archaeologist piece together the puzzle of the site he or she is working on, as we will see later.

As the years pass, new layers of humus cover up the older layers. If you were to leave a comic book on the forest floor and then return 20 years later, you would not be able to find the comic again without the help of a shovel!

It isn't just trees that create humus. In the Great Plains of North America, thousands of years' worth of humus from wild prairie grasses and crops cover archaeological sites.

◆ NATURAL DISASTERS

Volcanic eruptions can quickly cover hundreds of square miles of land with molten lava and a thick layer of hot, gray ash. This happened in 1980, when Mount Saint Helens erupted in Washington State, killing everything in the 50 square miles around it. Of course, the most famous eruption

happened 2,000 years ago in A.D. 79, when Mount Vesuvius erupted, covering the towns of Pompeii and Herculaneum and all of their inhabitants in 40 feet of mud, ash, and lava! These two towns remained lost under ash and mud until the 18th century. Even today, new sections of the towns are still being uncovered by archaeologists, several feet under the ground. How near to a volcano do you live? Most volcanoes in the Americas are along the West Coast, from Alaska down through Mexico to Chile and Peru.

Besides volcanic eruptions, floods can also cause whole villages to "sink" below ground level. When rivers flood their banks, a fine dirt called *silt* (found at river bottoms) is deposited over the land and left there after the water levels go down. After several floods, this silt can completely cover any traces of an ancient village.

Besides depositing soil, floods can cause *erosion*, the crumbling away of hillsides or rock slopes. Erosion tends to happen gradually. Once it has started, every storm or rainfall carries a little more dirt and rock down the slope.

On the other hand, windstorms can quickly cover sites, especially in the desert or along a beachfront, where lightweight grains of sand are

easily picked up by the wind. Shifting sands can even change the boundaries of where deserts begin and end.

Wind, rain, erosion, and earthquakes can happen in a matter of a few years. Now imagine all the change that can occur over millions of years. That is why the remains of our oldest ancestors are so far below the surface that only deep quarrying, natural gorges, or faults in the earth can reveal these artifacts.

◆ HUMAN INTERVENTION

Although nature is usually to blame for hiding archaeological sites, sometimes humans are the culprits. How so? What do people do that can hide a site? The answer is simple. Once people find a good place to live they tend to stay there. As old civilizations die out or leave, new people move in and often build their cities right on top of the ruins of the old inhabitants. In many cities, whenever a new skyscraper is built, archaeologists find remains from hundreds and even thousands of years ago. For example, smack in the middle of present-day Mexico City are newly found ruins of the ancient Aztec city of Tenochtitlán.

Ancient people did not have the convenience of using matches. They used rocks to start fires. Flint or quartz was often used, and pyrite was a good choice because it contains sulfur, the same flammable ingredient found on the tips of modern-day matches (and one of the reasons a match smells when you first light it). This activity should be done with a parent or adult supervisor.

MATERIALS

- ◆ *2 pieces of quartz or flint, or 1 piece of flint and 1 piece of pyrite*
- ◆ *Leather work gloves or garden gloves*
- ◆ *Plastic safety goggles*

Go outside when it is dark. With gloves and goggles on, strike one rock against the other. You should see a little blue or orange spark and maybe even smell a faint burning odor. Until a little more than a hundred years ago, flint was used to spark fires; and until recently it was still used in cigarette lighters.

Tool Makers

◆ Scientists classified the first toolmaker, the one who first struck one rock against another, as *Homo habilis* (Latin for "handy man"). *Homo habilis* is the first creature recognized as being in the human family, or genus. Any animal in the human family is referred to with the genus name *Homo*, followed by the species name. Do you know what scientists call modern humans?

Homo habilis first appeared about 2.5 million years ago and, from what archaeologists have found, used only crude chopper tools. In fact, some of these tools are so slightly changed, if you saw one on the ground today you would pass right by. So how can archaeologists tell that a rock is a tool?

A rock that has been struck by another rock will look different than a rock that has broken in half naturally. When you look at one of these early tools, you can see the place where the rock was hit, called the *striking platform*. Another way archaeologists can tell if a rock is a tool is by looking for signs of wear and damage around the edges. Sometimes this chipping is so slight it can only be seen under magnification. A final way archaeologists can tell a rock is a tool is by what else they find near these stones. Whenever bones of the *Homo habilis* are found, archaeologists carefully examine all the rocks they find nearby.

With patience, archaeologists can also identify hammerstones, the rocks used to strike other rocks and make tools.

These *Homo habilis* may have used wooden tools also, but wood does not last as well as rock does, as you will see later on. Since the earliest tools we have found so far are all made of stone, the era when *Homo habilis* lived is known as the Paleolithic, from the Latin for "Old Stone Age." The Paleolithic lasted more than two million years, and is divided into three periods: Lower (oldest), Middle, and Upper (most recent).

The earliest tools were either *core tools* or *flake tools*. A core tool is a tool made from the rock that is being struck, like a hammer or a hand ax. A flake tool is made from the piece of rock that flakes off the stone that is being struck.

Though the first hominids were limited to Africa, another group eventually spread out through Europe and Asia, something *Homo habilis* or Australopithecus had never accomplished. These smarter creatures were known as *Homo erectus*, Latin for "Upright Man." Erectus could make an improved kind of tool, called a hand ax, which was more useful than a chopper. The hand ax was usually pear-shaped, and finely chiseled so it had more regular edges. Now that our distant relatives had sharper tools, they could skin animals and use the hides for clothing; and around that time, these early hominids also discovered how to start and control fires. Both of

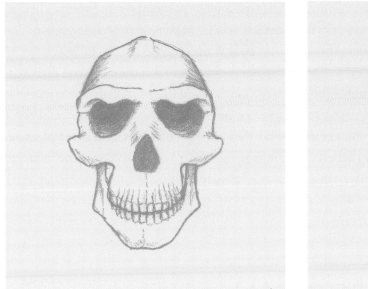 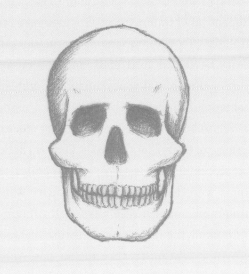

▲ *A* Homo erectus *skull (left) and a modern human skull (right).*

these discoveries were necessary for *Homo erectus* to survive in the cold climate of Northern Europe and Northern Asia.

Finding Remains

◆ At first, archaeologists did not believe that the skeletons and tools they were finding in Asia, Europe, and Africa were part of the same species. The first *Homo erectus* remains were found on the Indonesian island of Java by Eugene Dubois in 1890, but at the time Dubois referred to them scientifically as *Pithecanthropus erectus,* though most people called them Java Man. Similar remains found in China during the 1920s were called *Sinanthropus pekinensis,* or Peking Man. A German *Homo erectus* (found in 1907) was called *Homo heidelbergensis,* after the city of Heidelberg, which was six miles from where the remains were found in a commercial sand pit.

In 1908, an English lawyer and amateur archaeologist named Charles Dawson found some bits of bones from the skull of a humanlike creature near Piltdown Common, Sussex County, England, after finding some flint tools on a casual stroll down a country lane. Over the next three years, he found flint tools and several other human and animal bones, including prehistoric mastodon, horse, and beaver. This seemed to prove the humanlike bones were very old, as old as those of the ancient animals. Dawson believed the pieces of jaw, teeth, eye socket, and other bones were from the same creature. When a famous anatomist pieced together the fragments of the skull, the result was a creature that looked human, except for its very apelike jaw. Another odd thing about the fossil was that the brain was very large, about the same as a modern human's. Scientists were divided in their opinions of this newly named *Eoanthropus dawsoni*, or "Dawson's Dawn Man" in Latin. Some thought it was the "missing link" between the apes and modern humans. Others were uncertain that the bits of bone even belonged to the same species of creature.

For more than 35 years, the Piltdown Mystery was unsolved. Many people spent a lot of time researching and writing about Piltdown Man, trying to prove their theories. Then, in 1949, new tests showed that the Eoanthropus bones were only about 50,000 years old, while the other animal bones were much older. A few years later, another test was done on the jaw and on the rest of the skull showing they were of different ages

and could not be part of the same animal. In fact, the jaw was probably that of an orangutan!

Who was responsible for the Piltdown Hoax? No one is quite sure. Charles Dawson died suddenly in 1916, and there is still debate about who was to blame. Was Dawson just a bored lawyer who thought he could become famous as an archaeologist? Or was it an innocent mistake, maybe planted for him to find by someone else?

Modern Human Relatives

◆ Unlike the disappointment of Piltdown, most of the other bones that were being found were real. Once technology allowed scientists to compare the ages of the rest of the ancient tools and skulls that had been found, and they decided that Peking Man, Java Man, and many of the other recently found remains belonged to one ancestor of modern humans that they called *Homo erectus*.

Since the 1950s, there has been another change in the classification of *Homo erectus*. Scientists have now separated the African, Asian, and European *Homo erectus* back into different species. The earliest *Homo erectus*, the one that lived in Africa, is now known as *Homo erganster*. The Asian fossils are now called *Homo erectus*, while the European fossils are now called *Homo heidelbergensis*.

These three species were very successful, and combined they lasted more than one and a half million years! As time passed, the tools they produced became more delicate. Instead of just a few strikes, these later stone tools were struck repeatedly so the entire surface was worked over. The shape of the hand axes became thinner and sharper. At this point, a *Homo erectus* must have realized that such a stone could be attached to a long, straight branch of wood and used as a spear. Of course, all that remains today of these first spears are the stone tips.

Why do you think spears were such good weapons? Well, for one thing, they could hit a moving target or a dangerous animal from a safe distance. Imagine trying to kill a woolly mammoth singlehandedly! A few hunters with spears could do the job and actually come out of it in one piece.

During the Middle Paleolithic, a new species emerged called *Homo sapiens neanderthalensis*. These "Neanderthals" were named after a valley in Germany where they were first found in 1856, during a limestone quarrying operation. The workers were going to get rid of the bones but the quarry owner found out and saved them. Though they looked more like humans than *Homo habilis*

or *Homo erectus*, they still did not look exactly like modern humans. Neanderthals had no chins or foreheads; their heads sloped back above their eyes. They also had a very large brow ridge. Feel the bone jutting just above your eyebrows. Now imagine that ridge being so prominent that when you look in the mirror it is the first thing you notice!

Though we sometimes refer to primitive-looking or acting people as Neanderthals, the real Neanderthals had larger brains than ours! In 1908 an old Neanderthal man's skeleton was found, protected by stones and surrounded by stone tools. More recently, archaeologist Ralph Solecki found evidence in a cave in Iraq that Neanderthals may have believed in religion and afterlife, and buried their dead with daisies and other flowers. They also cared for sick and weak family members, something that did not happen with *Homo habilis* and *Homo erectus*. What do you think the advantages were for the Neanderthals to take care of an old, handicapped man who could no longer hunt? What can we learn from our own grandparents or great-grandparents who are no longer able to move around very well?

On the other hand, archaeologists now think they have definite evidence that some Neanderthals practiced cannibalism. New evidence of Neanderthal bones mixed in with deer bones suggests this was true. From the patterns of scrape marks on the bones, archaeologists can tell that

Measuring Brain Capacity

How can scientists tell how large an ancient brain was when all they have to work with is an empty skull?

MATERIALS

- ◆ *Plastic skull (like the kind you might find around Halloween, or maybe a more realistic one from a science/learning store)*
- ◆ *5 pounds (2.3 kg) of sand (you can also use granulated sugar or birdseed)*
- ◆ *Rectangular or square clear plastic box or container*
- ◆ *Ruler*
- ◆ *Calculator*

Hold the skull upside down and fill the skull with sand about up to the eye level. Carefully pour the sand from the skull into the plastic container and be sure the surface is level. Measure the width, length, and height of the sand in centimeters. Now multiply the three numbers. This is the brain size in cubic centimeters (cc). How does this compare with a gorilla or an Austalopithecus (about 450 cc) or *Homo erectus* (900–1000 cc)? Is it anywhere near the size of a normal modern human brain (1300–1400 cc)?

▲ *An example of a flake tool, about 60,000 years old.*

An exhibit on how flake tools were made. ▶

the meat was deliberately scraped off the bone with a sharp object. The only animal capable of doing this would have been a Neanderthal.

Evidence of cannibalism has not been found very often and most people believe that overall, most Neanderthals were socially advanced. Besides this, they had made new technological advances in toolmaking. Archaeologists have found advanced flake tools at Neanderthal sites. Instead of throwing away the pieces of rock that were chipped off when they made large tools, like

axes, the Neanderthals took these flakes and used a pointy antler or strong piece of bone to pressure flake off small edges, making the flake a sharp tool itself.

Flake tools are much easier to identify than core tools. A core tool can look like an ordinary rock, but a flake tool has probably been chipped at several times, leaving distinct fracture marks. Each type of stone fractures differently. Flint, chert, quartz, agate, and jasper are all members of the quartz family, and have a *conchoidal*, or shell-like, fracture. When archaeologists see these circle-within-a-circle patterns on the edges of rocks, they can be pretty sure that they have found ancient flake tools.

As humanlike creatures moved forward in time, they were able to make still better tools. While the *Homo habilis* and early *Homo erectus* only used one basic tool type, the later *Homo sapiens* species had specialized tool kits, much like what you might find in your home. Each tool had a different job. There were scrapers, drills, blades, miniature saws, and chisels. The first true humans could adapt to their environment very well and make tools for whatever they needed. You might remember that the first *Homo* species emerged about 2,500,000 years ago. Well, it took about 2,450,000 years for the species known as *Homo sapiens sapiens* (Latin for "Thinking Man") to first come into existence. Look in the mirror and you will hopefully see a *Homo sapiens sapiens* staring back at you!

▲ *A conchoidal fracture is commonly seen in stone tools made of any mineral in the quartz family. It is also seen on glass and its volcanic cousin, obsidian.*

The First Humans

◆ *Homo sapiens sapiens*, or humans, continued to do well after the last Neanderthals mysteriously died out about 30,000 years ago. Humans were widespread all across Africa, Asia, and Europe, and sometime between 15,000 and 20,000 years ago crossed the Bering Strait land bridge from Asia into the Americas.

This species was so smart they could create artworks, sew clothing with needle and thread,

Generations

If each of us is indeed descended from early Homo sapiens sapiens, *how many generations removed would we be from the first modern humans?*

Over the last 50,000 years, a generation was on average 20 years—in the early days, life spans were shorter and people had children at a younger age—probably even younger than 20. Using a calculator, divide 50,000 by 20 to come up with the number of generations that separate us from the first people.

To figure out the average generation in your family, write down the ages your parents were when you were born, and then the ages their parents were when they were born, and further back, if you can get that information. Add up all the ages you have written down and divide it by the number of people whose ages you have written down. This is the average number of years between generations in your family.

▲ *As toolmaking skills increased, human ancestors were able to make better tools by flaking the edges more precisely.*

and hunt with bow and arrow. Humans and Neanderthals may have coexisted in the same places for a short time, but in the end, humans survived and Neanderthals did not. They were almost modern in appearance; in fact, you might not even notice if one of these early *Homo sapiens*

sapiens—also known as Cro-Magnon—was walking down the street right in front of you!), they were still living in the Stone Age. That was about to change quickly as the last great Ice Age came to a close, as you will read in Chapter 3.

◇-◇

Stone Tools

For thousands and thousands of years, our ancestors had to use tools made from stones they found lying around their campsites. At first, they simply used the stones as they found them, but as they got smarter, they began to change the shape of the stones by striking them against other stones. They discovered that tools of a certain shape and size were good for specific tasks. In this activity, you will pretend to be an early human and see how tools made life easier.

MATERIALS

◆ *5 or 6 stones of different sizes and shapes, between roughly 3 inches (8 cm) and 10 inches (30 cm) in length*
◆ *Sheet of paper*
◆ *6 unshelled peanuts*
◆ *Large handful of fresh corn kernels*
◆ *Square of cotton fabric (from an old T-shirt you don't need—get permission first!)*
◆ *Brick*

Line up these items on a hard outdoor surface, preferably concrete or asphalt. With each stone, go down the line and try to cut the paper, crack a peanut shell, grind the corn into a mush, and cut the T-shirt fabric. Be careful not to hurt yourself! What stone shape and size is best for each activity? What changes do you think early people might have made to these stones to make them easier to use?

Now take the brick and go down the line with each of the items. Can the man-made brick do any of the tasks better than the stones you found?

The Ice Age and the New Stone Age

3

Imagine the temperature where you live is 20 degrees colder throughout the year, and imagine that many of the plants and animals that once lived nearby have died off. Summers are shorter and cooler. Fall and spring feel more like winter. Now imagine the only heat you have is from fire, and you have to wrap yourself in animal skins to keep warm. Imagine you do not have a house to live in, and the only place that can offer you some shelter from the frozen winds is a hut or, if you are lucky, a cave.

This is what it was like for our human ancestors during the last great Ice Age, between 40,000 and 10,000 years ago. Massive sheets of ice, called glaciers, covered as much as 30 percent of the world. The movement of these glaciers, weighing thousands and thousands of tons each, created many of the hills and valleys in Canada, the northern parts of the United States, and Europe. While our ancestors must have had a difficult time during the Ice Age, their large brains

Ice Archaeology

When a European hiker recently stumbled across a frozen ice-man now known as Oetzi, it excited archaeologists all over the world. Because he was frozen, Oetzi, his clothes, and his possessions were well preserved—even after more than 5,000 years. What kinds of things are preserved well in ice? What happens after they are defrosted?

MATERIALS

- *4 clear plastic cups (at least 8 ounces)*
- *Small piece of newspaper (about 1 inch × 1 inch)*
- *Pebble*
- *Piece of bread*
- *Blueberry, currant, or other small fruit*
- *Small nail (also called a finishing nail)*
- *Metal paper clip*
- *Small leaf*
- *Tweezers*
- *Pencil*
- *Sheet of paper*

Place the paper into one cup, the bread and the blueberry into another cup, the nail and paper clip into a third cup, and the leaf into the fourth cup. Now, fill each cup ¾ of the way with water and place them in the freezer. Use the pebbles to keep the paper, bread, and leaf from floating to the surface.

After four days, remove the cups from the freezer. When the ice has melted, remove the objects with the tweezers. Discard the pebbles.

Write down the condition of each of the objects. Have any of them changed? Without drying the objects off at all, place each of them in a dry, bright place. After another four days, look at their condition. How do they look, compared to when they were frozen?

While ice is a great preserver, the frozen artifacts will not last long unless they are kept away from moisture, heat, and sunlight. The ice Oetzi was buried in was just beginning to melt when the hiker found him. If Oetzi hadn't been found at that time, he might not have lasted much longer. After archaeologists carefully removed him from the ice, Oetzi and his frozen possessions had to be studied in a special climate-controlled place so they did not crumble into dust.

helped them find shelter, make new tools, and outsmart large animals so they could have food to eat.

The Big Freeze

◆ As each Ice Age began, ocean levels began to go down as liquid water turned to massive sheets of ice. The ice advanced south over land as the weather got colder. As it pushed its way south, animals and human ancestors were forced to move further south. Trees and plants were crushed and killed by the glaciers. The air above the ice became dry—there was little water evaporating because it was so cold—and there was less and less snow. The forests, with their need for moisture and their warmth-loving plants, died from the dry and windy cold. Because there was little snow feeding the ice, it began to melt very slowly at its southern edges, helped by the sun's radiant heat. The ice receded very slowly, less than nine inches per day, but gradually retreated to the far northern regions where it is normally found today. As the glaciers melted, evaporation started again. Year after year snow fell, compressed, and froze, becoming part of the glaciers. Over time, the massive ice sheets built up and pushed their way south once more. This cycle has

repeated four times during the last million years, and though some scientists worry about global warming, nobody knows for sure if we are headed for another Ice Age in the near future!

As the ice pushed south each time, just ahead of it were cold but inhabitable conditions. The mostly frozen land was known as *tundra*. On the tundra, only a few inches of the ground would thaw out during the warmer months, making it impossible for trees or large plants to root. Instead, only small plants like lichens, mosses, and some grasses and flowers could survive. Great herds of prehistoric animals roamed the tundra in search of food.

▲ *Tundra still exists today in the northern latitudes and at high altitudes. This photo shows the sparse vegetation near the top of Pike's Peak, Colorado.*

While animals had thick coats of fur, people weren't so lucky. The only way for them to keep warm was with fires, and archaeologists have uncovered thousands of prehistoric *hearths*, or fireplaces. Some of these hearths contained the remains of food, bits of wood used for kindling, and scraps of tools. Because the weather was so cold, Ice Age people had to keep their fires burn-

Building a Paleolithic Fireplace

One of the biggest steps in the development of our human ancestors was the control of fire. Once they could start fires, Homo erectus and Homo sapiens could cook meat, keep away wild animals, and most importantly, stay warm. They could also use fire as a way to see through the darkness of long winter nights. Think how unpleasant it would be living in a cave without any light.

A fire could not simply be built in an open space, as our ancestors might have learned the hard way. In order to get a warm and safe night's sleep by a fire, there had to be a way to control the flames. Early humans noticed that wood and plants burned easily, but stones and clay did not. A hearth, or stone fireplace, was the simplest way to keep a fire burning. Stones could also absorb heat and release it slowly, even after the fire died. Because a hearth is made of stones, which do not decompose, it is also easily found by archaeologists.

MATERIALS
- 10–20 large, relatively flat stones (slate would be good)
- 20 oblong or round stones
- Trowel or small shovel

Find a place outdoors, a backyard or a beach for example, and lay the flat stones next to one another in a circular pattern. Now, plant the rounded stones, one by one, around the outer edge of the circle of flat stones to form a border. Dig a little so that each stone is about halfway in the ground. You have now built a paleolithic hearth.

When early people moved their camps, what do you think happened to their hearths?

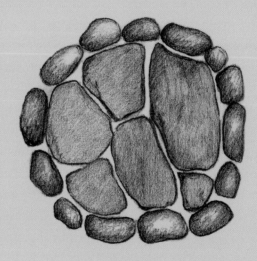

ing whenever they were not moving around. Fire also served another purpose, to keep wolves and other wild animals away. If you went out to hunt and lost your way, the smoke from a distant fire could guide you back to safety and warmth. Can you imagine sitting around a prehistoric fireplace at night, trading stories with the others about the adventures of the day?

How Do Archaeologists Know How Old Something Is?

The first humanlike creatures walked the earth more than two million years ago, but how do we know that? In fact, how do we know anything about the age of any stone tool or skeleton? The first archaeologists had little help in figuring out the age of their discoveries, but with modern technology, there are many different ways to date something. Most of these dating methods are possible because of tiny changes in rocks, plants, and animals that happen when thousands and millions of years go by.

Imagine you have buried a block of uranium in your backyard. If you forgot about it for a few hundred million years, when you returned to get it, there would only be half as much as you buried. The other half would have converted into something else. Uranium, along with many other elements, is radioactive. This means it is not stable,

as a block of gold would be for the same amount of time. Chemical changes take place and the unstable uranium converts to stable lead. The time it takes for half of the mass of a radioactive material to convert is called its half-life.

Archaeologists can use radioactive materials to figure out the age of something they have found by measuring the amount of radioactive potassium in rocks nearby. When the Leakeys found Homo habilis remains in Africa, potassium-argon dating (the unstable radioactive element potassium becomes the stable gas argon) could be used on the rock formations where the bones were found. By measuring how much argon was in the rocks, scientists could figure out how old the volcanic rocks were, and make a good guess at the age of the bones. The half-life of potassium is more than one billion years, so this method is only

good for very old rocks, since it takes at least 100,000 years for enough argon to be made that can it be measured.

Living creatures on earth are carbon-based. In your body there is both regular carbon and radioactive carbon. When a plant or animal dies, the amount of regular carbon remains the same while the amount of radioactive carbon goes down as it decays and becomes the gas nitrogen. Carbon dating measures the amount of radioactive carbon left in the remains to determine when something died. The wood from a 1,000-year-old house could be tested to see when the tree was cut down. However, a 100-year-old house would not be a good candidate for this kind of dating because the amount of carbon that has decayed will be too small to measure accurately.

Cave Dwellers

◆ For many early people, caves provided a convenient place to live. Archaeologists have found evidence of cave dwellers all across Europe. These cave sites are often well preserved because they remained sealed and untouched for thousands of years. But just because early humans lived in caves, it does not mean they were not very advanced.

The cave dwellers, beginning with the Neanderthals mentioned earlier, showed signs of being very intelligent. They made and used a wide variety of tools and were expert hunters. Some of the earliest evidence of ancient art is also found in caves, where archaeologists and explorers have uncovered spectacular paintings of animals and human figures. At first, almost nobody believed these paintings could have been made by Paleolithic people. How could these primitive people make such beautiful paintings? After scientific dating of the artifacts found in the caves, archaeologists had proof that most of the paintings were more than 10,000 years old.

The most famous cave art was discovered by a young boy at Lascaux, France, in 1940, and depicts more than 500 painted animals. The 17,000-year-old paintings of Lascaux were such a popular tourist attraction that the cave paintings were starting to get damaged from all the moisture of human breath from the thousands of visitors who took tours there every year. This cave was closed in 1963, and others may be closed to the public for good so that they can be preserved for future generations to study.

Besides Lascaux, more than 150 other caves with paintings inside have been discovered around Europe and Africa. These paintings show horses, bison, deer, rhinoceri, and mammoths in many colors. The paint was usually made from finely crushed rocks. One of the most common paints was made from ochre, a mixture of clay and minerals, to make reddish, yellow, orange, and brown colors.

Why did ancient people paint on the walls of their caves? There is much speculation about it. The most simple answer is that these people wanted to have some decoration in these dark, dreary caves in which they spent long, cold winter nights. This could be true, but there may have been other reasons.

Many of the paintings show animals being killed by human hunters, animals with bloody spear wounds, and animals running from hunters' spears. Maybe by showing these events happening, the cave dwellers thought they could make them come true. This idea is called *sympathetic magic*. By painting these animals, the cave dwellers may have thought they were capturing and controlling the animals' spirits, making it easier to hunt and kill them. This might explain why archaeologists almost never find realistic paintings of humans in any of these caves. If you thought painting something or someone was magic, and would capture its spirit or put it in danger, would you paint a friend or family member?

There are still many mysteries surrounding cave art. We can never be quite positive what purpose they served; but they were painted using powdered minerals mixed with animal fat to make them waterproof, so we know the artists intended them to last a long time and not just fade away.

Cave paintings are not the only form of early art. In fact, archaeologists around the world have found clay sculptures of animals, carved animal bones, and carved mammoth tusks that go even farther back in time than the cave paintings. All of these materials are likely to be found by archaeologists after thousands of years because they survive well over time.

The ancient sculptures and etchings became more and more sophisticated over the years. Sometimes they represented actual animals, and sometimes they represented mythical creatures,

Early art usually featured animals. In this photograph of prehistoric paintings at Nswatungi Cave in the African country of Zimbabwe, you can see human and animal figures. ▶

half human and half animal. When archaeologists find ancient art, it is a window into ancient peoples' hearts and minds. Since these early humans did not have written language, art gives us our best clues into what they were thinking and feeling.

<hr>

Cave Art

While most cave art does not show actual people in any detail, there have been many stick figures and outlines of human hands found in caves across Europe. In this game you will try to outline your hand using a technique the cave dwellers may have used. While pictures of animals could easily have been painted by using fingers or maybe a crude brush, the "negative" hand image was most likely created using paint blown through a bone pipe.

MATERIALS
◆ *Stone (about the size of your fist)*
◆ *Dish detergent*
◆ *2 handfuls of ripe blackberries or blueberries*
◆ *Piece of cardboard about the size of this book*
◆ *Vegetable or olive oil*
◆ *Drinking straw*
◆ *Large sheet (or two) of light-colored construction paper*
◆ *Twig (optional)*
◆ *Clump of moss or grass (optional)*

Scrub the stone well with dish detergent and rinse it off. Take a handful of berries and place them on the cardboard. Using the stone, mash the berries until they are completely mushy and messy. Now, add a few of drops of vegetable oil to bind the "paint" to the construction paper. Stir with the straw. Now, take some onto one end of the straw and bring the other end to your mouth with one hand. Place your other hand on the construction paper, and aim at the edge of your hand. Now blow hard through the straw. Get more paint (but don't move your modeling hand!) and blow again. Keep going until you have "painted" the outline of your hand. It could take a few minutes.

If you want to try another method of cave painting, get a twig and a clump of moss or a small (2-inch square) clump of grass. Dip the twig in the "paint" and draw the outline of an animal on construction paper. Now dip the moss in the paint and pat inside of the animal's outline.

Early Hunters

◆ Cave art was only possible where there were caves, and of course, caves are not found everywhere in the world. It just happens that southern France and Spain have many naturally occurring caves. Elsewhere, the Ice Age people had to seek other shelter. For example, on the flatlands of northern Europe and Russia, the hunters had to build huts out of whatever materials were available, including mammoth bones for walls and hard-to-find thin tree branches for roofs.

Another sign of Upper Paleolithic people's intelligence was in their crafty way of hunting animals. Archaeologists have found thousands of horse skeletons at the bottom of a cliff in France, suggesting that ancient hunters would tease and coax the animals in the direction of the cliff, causing a stampede. The thousand-foot fall would easily kill the animals and provide enough meat for everyone in the tribe.

For large animals such as mammoths and reindeer, barbed spears and harpoons were used. Even as far back in time as the Neanderthals, archaeologists have found evidence of bear being hunted on a regular basis. It must have taken quick wits and great strength to outsmart and kill these huge, dangerous animals.

Early Farmers

◆ Humans lived through the cold for more than 30,000 years, until about 10,000 years ago, when the Ice Age finally ended and the glaciers retreated northward. People could once again live in places the ice had covered for so long. The end of the last Ice Age marked the beginning of a period European archaeologists refer to as the Mesolithic ("Middle Stone Age"). The world's climate was actually a little bit warmer than it is today. New animals and dense forests flourished. Gone were the large mastodons, woolly mammoths, prehistoric rhinoceros, and sabertooth tigers. Instead, there were lots of deer and smaller forest animals. The Mesolithic people had new and improved tools, many of them small and precise. These microliths could easily be carried from place to place. The Mesolithic people could sew clothing using bone needles. Warmer temperatures meant plant life was plentiful and people probably relied on grains, berries, nuts, and roots more than ever. The Mesolithic was definitely a time of transition, and it was around this time humans first experimented with agriculture.

For thousands of years, ancient people had been gathering nuts, fruits, roots, and other parts of plants to eat. One day, somebody noticed that where plants dropped their fruit or seeds in the

Microliths, from the Latin for "tiny stones," were miniature tools that could be used by themselves or combined for more effective use.

MATERIALS

- ◆ *Clay (the kind that hardens)*
- ◆ *Straight stick or dowel, about 12 inches long*
- ◆ *All-purpose white glue*
- ◆ *Pencil, sharpened (or ball-point pen)*

Break off five small balls of clay, each about one inch in diameter. Shape each one by pinching it until it is a long, flat, triangular shape. Using a pencil point, make one side of one of the pieces jagged by scraping away bits of clay. Leave the five pieces out and let them harden. When they are hard, lay the stick down on some newspaper. Next, put glue on one of the long sides of each clay piece. Attach two next to each other on one side of the stick and three on the other side. Make sure the jagged piece is at the very top, so its tip is touching the tip of the stick. Now let the glue dry.

You have made a model of a hunting weapon similar to what archaeologists have found! Archaeologists believe this microlith was used as a spear.

fall was where new plants sprouted in the spring. Or maybe people noticed that once in a while a few of the seeds or nuts they had gathered, after lying around for too long, began to germinate and tiny green leaves began to appear. "Hey!" they must have thought, "This is great! If we gather some seeds and scatter them near our huts, then maybe we won't have to walk so far to get food!" By clearing land around their homes, they could make room for growing the crops they wanted to eat.

The New Stone Age

◆ Not long after the Mesolithic came the Neolithic, or New Stone Age. This exciting time saw many changes in peoples' way of life. Neolithic people were skilled at using clay to make pottery. They were now becoming expert farmers and lived in budding communities of more than 5,000 people. Archaeologists have shown that only in places where there was agriculture did populations reach such high numbers. Think about how difficult it would be to feed 5,000 people based on hunting and gathering alone. That would be an awful lot of time spent looking for roots, berries, and wild vegetables to pick.

Still, agriculture was not the only source of food for Neolithic people. They also relied on the domestication of animals. Instead of hunting dozens of wild animals every day, they learned how to take wild animals and keep them fenced in, breeding the tamest ones together. In some animals, our ancestors found other traits that were desirable. People learned they could encour-

▲ *Tools were made of stone, bone, and wood and had a wide variety of uses. Shown here are Native American tools on display at the Garvies Point Museum in Glen Cove, New York.*

age these traits by breeding only those animals that had the desirable traits. Sheep with short legs, they found, would be less likely to jump over fences and could not run very fast. Heavy pigs were better than lean, scrawny ones. Allowing only certain animals to breed gave people control over how their herds looked and behaved. What kinds of animals do farmers keep today?

How do archaeologists know when they have found a site where domestication has taken place? By the number and type of animal bones found. Sometimes, the changes in animal bones

Experimenting with Agriculture

Growing crops was a better way to feed many people than relying on plants that could be found in nature. By controlling the spacing of the seeds and the amount of sunlight and water that plants received, more people could be fed.

In this experiment, you will try your hand at agriculture as people first did 10,000 years ago.

MATERIALS

- ◇ *5 egg cartons*
- ◇ *Soil*
- ◇ *Plastic spoon*
- ◇ *Various seeds, five different kinds (They could include green peppers, green beans, oranges, grapefruits, grapes, cucumbers, squash, and anything else you can find, such as oak or maple acorns—but remember, the*

first farmers didn't have mail-order seed catalogs! They gathered seeds from fruits and plants themselves, so get yours from trees and plants in your neighborhood, and from fruits and vegetables in your supermarket.)

Dry the seeds well for a week or two. Fill the egg carton compartments with soil and plant a couple of seeds in each compartment, about half an inch deep. Water a little bit every day and put in a sunny place. Watch the progress as they grow into seedlings. Which seeds did the best? Remember, the first farmers had to take these tiny seedlings and keep them growing for months until the plants could be used for food!

Your little plants cannot survive in those egg containers forever. For one thing, the compartments are too small for the growing root systems of these baby plants. For another, the plants' roots absorb the nutrients in the soil, and after a while, the soil is drained. Early farmers learned this lesson, too. They developed a system to let some fields lie empty, or fallow, once in a while. This allowed the soil to rest and regain some of its nutrients for the next time it was planted. If you'd like, transplant your seedlings into larger pots.

After a thousand years of using the same fields, even with crop rotation and field sharing, soils can still be depleted of nutrients beyond help. Archaeologists have found remains of civilizations that thrived for a long time and then suddenly disappeared, such as the Mohenjo-Daro people of Asia. In that case, it is possible the soil was too exhausted to support life any more.

over time can tell us a lot of information about what was happening in the society.

One of the most famous Neolithic towns ever discovered is Çatal Höyük, found in Turkey in 1958 by the archaeologist James Mellaart. This town featured attached buildings made of mud bricks. Each house or apartment had a fireplace, an oven, and a bench. There were no doors in this community. Access to each house was only possible through the roof. Dating to 6500 B.C., it is one of the best and earliest examples of people who farmed and bred animals for food.

Every Neolithic site is different, but each one shows signs of people who were technologically advanced. On the island of Malta, for example, the elaborately decorated stones of the Tarxien Temple show that highly skilled craftsmen worked long hours to achieve their goals. At the famous site of Lepinski Vir, along the Danube River in Serbia, archaeologists have found 7,000-year-old carved symbols that could be a very early attempt at a form of writing. During the Neolithic, people continued to use art as a way to express themselves and make their surroundings a little more beautiful. At Lepinski Vir, archaeologists uncovered large stone sculptures in front of the inhabitants' houses, and some of the earliest sculptures of human faces in all of Europe.

Because most Neolithic people were *sedentary* (staying in one place) as opposed to *migratory* (moving with the changing seasons), they were

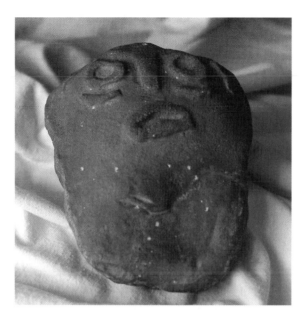

◄ *Cast of a stone face sculpture found at the Neolithic site of Lepinski Vir.*

The Yang Shao culture in China was known for its painted pottery with black stripes or swirls. ▼

able to create many more personal objects and vessels for food storage and cooking. If they had to pack up all their belongings every few months, it would not make sense to have so many pots, jars, trinkets, and tools. As Neolithic people became experts in using clay and making pots,

Animal Bones

Finding animal remains at an archaeological site can give us many clues about the diet and lifestyle of the people who once lived there. In this activity, you will calculate the percentages of different animal bones on an island we'll call Terraledge, and try to come to some conclusions. The only thing archaeologists knew about the people before the excavations began was that as time passed, they moved from the west end of the island to the east end.

MATERIALS
◆ Pencil
◆ Paper
◆ Calculator

To figure out the percentage of the Terraledgers' diet represented by each animal, first add together the total of all bones and shells found at each site.

Then, divide the number of remains found for each animal by the total. For example, if you divide 50 elk remains by a total number of 100 remains, you get an answer of .5. Then multiply by 100 to get the percentage: .5 × 100 = 50. The answer is, 50 percent (%) of the remains were elk. Round all answers to the nearest percentage.

SITES SURVEYED	A–WEST	B–MIDDLE	C–EAST
Wild Goose	200	100	50
Goat	0	100	1,000
Bear	500	300	50
Elk	400	200	100
Rabbit	20	100	500
Sheep	20	200	800

What happened to the people's diet as they moved from one side of the island to the other?

Can you tell what happened to the population of Terraledge as time went by? As an experiment, take note of what foods you eat and how much of them you eat for lunch and dinner for a week. What is the most common food item in YOUR diet?

ANSWERS:

SITE A—Total remains 1,140; Goose 18%, Goat 0%, Bear 44%, Elk 35%, Rabbit 2%, Sheep 2%

SITE B—Total remains 1,000; Goose 10%, Goat 10%, Bear 30%, Elk 20%, Rabbit 10%, Sheep 20%

SITE C—Total remains 2,500; Goose 2%, Goat 40%, Bear 2%, Elk 4%, Rabbit 20%, Sheep 32%

It appears that as the people moved from one side of the island to the other, they relied less on large, wild animals and more on smaller wild and domesticated animals. This could mean these people were beginning to develop agriculture.

▲ *Stonehenge was first built more than 4,000 years ago during the Neolithic period in England and used for astronomical observations.*

The Stone Age is a term often used for the time period when advanced prehistoric people existed. In reality, Neolithic and Paleolithic refer more to the technological state of a particular group of people than to a specific time period. Not all people were at the same stage of development 7,000 years ago. The same held true for thousands of years. In fact, up until the mid-1900s, there were isolated groups of people scattered around the world who were still living a Stone Age lifestyle. As modern life expanded into all corners of the earth, these people's old ways gradually mixed with modern technology. It started with small things like trinkets and pots, and before long many of these people were either lured or forced into modern cities, giving up their old way of life as their villages disintegrated.

jars, bottles, bowls, and plates, they also began to decorate these items. Do your plates and bowls have designs on them? People have been decorating their "kitchenware," the containers they eat from and store food in, for more than 7,000 years! Perhaps Neolithic people realized if they were going to be using these items on an everyday basis they should be pleasing to the eye. In Neolithic China, a group called the Yang Shao culture is well known by archaeologists for their red clay pottery with black painted swirls and stripes.

Neolithic people were very ingenious. They began to experiment with creating megalithic, or "giant stone," structures. Some were tombs and others were religious or ceremonial sites. Archaeologists have found that the famous Stonehenge in England was built more than 4,000 years ago. Luckily, because the Neolithic was not that long ago, and because it was after the last Ice Age, in

▲ *This barren part of the western coast of Ireland, known as the Burren, was host to many prehistoric people. Archaeologists have found many stone tombs and other remains over the years.*

some unpopulated places there has not been too much change to the land over the last few thousand years. The eerie, gray region of western Ireland known as the Burren was home to many Neolithic people who built megalithic tombs and whose artifacts are still easily located by archaeologists.

As the populations of these Neolithic towns kept growing, there would have to be some drastic changes in their societies. No longer could people only use stone as their main material. Clay, wood, and various metals would be used to make tools, containers, artworks, and jewelry. Clothing for all these people could not simply be made from animal skins anymore—can you imagine how many beavers or deer it would take to clothe 5,000 to 10,000 people? Weavers would have to learn how to make fabric from wool or plant fibers like cotton or hemp. The largest Neolithic towns were filled with specialists who worked at one type of job. Some people were farmers, some were weavers, some were in charge of milling the grain, and some were expert artists. People traded different goods with each other, and with other towns dozens or even hundreds of miles away.

Many of these Neolithic towns would collapse or disappear when they grew too large. Fighting, floods, drought, or disease would finish them off. A few other bustling Neolithic towns continued to grow successfully. These towns were on the verge of becoming *civilizations*.

4 The First Civilizations

The best-known man-made structures of the last 5,000 years would have to be the pyramids in Egypt. These monumental structures, triangular in shape with a square base, were built to house dead pharaohs and some of the items they would need in the afterlife. If you go anywhere in the world, people are likely to have seen pictures or at least heard of the majestic Pyramids. For thousands of years, people have wondered how they were built.

▲ **Tourists have been flocking to the pyramids for hundreds of years. This photo shows a group of tourists and their guides about 100 years ago.**

How could ancient Egyptians have assembled more than two million stone blocks into the perfect Pyramid of Cheops? Even if they could have built a perfect base, how were they able keep building upward, to a final height of 480 feet? How were they able to get the top point of the pyramid to be exactly above the center point of the base without modern technology? Over the years, archaeologists and others have tried to calculate how many workers were needed and how long it would have taken. Some have even suggested that it wouldn't have been possible for humans to build the Great Pyramids without help from aliens from outer space!

So how were the Egyptians able to build such huge monuments?

The answer is civilization.

◇◇◇◇◇◇◇◇◇◇◇◇◇◇◇◇◇◇◇◇◇◇

Imagine you live in a house in a city of several thousand people. You and your parents had to fight for some land and then build your house yourselves. There are no laws or rules and nobody to stop you from doing whatever you want. There are no police to protect you from thieves, thugs, and murderers. There are no public roads, only private highways that you have to pay to drive along in your horse-drawn cart. Since there is no real money, you have to pay with whatever valuables you might have. Of course, there are no taxes, but you have to dispose of your own garbage and dig your own well for drinking water. There are also no schools for you to attend, so you probably do not know how to read or write. Only the very wealthy people in your town know how to read and write. Naturally, there are no museums or public libraries. There is no mail delivery. You can only send messages if you pay somebody to carry them. It would probably not be wise to spend too much time in the dirt streets because there are no sewers to carry your wastewater, so most of it winds up in a big stinky mess on the muddy roads. When you get sick, don't expect much help because there aren't any hospitals, and only the rich and powerful can afford doctors. If you want to leave town and cross a river, forget it, because there are no bridges. There are no office buildings or skyscrapers, no railroads, and no airplanes. If another group of people invaded your town and tried to take over, they might succeed because there is no army to defend your territory. All in all, city life is not really possible if you are living in an uncivilized society.

As you saw in the last chapter, Neolithic towns were getting larger by 4000 B.C., their populations growing into the tens of thousands. During this time, they started to experiment with each of the different components of civilization. They created organized governments to watch and protect the rights of the people, build roads, and oversee the distribution of food. These governments made city life possible.

Because ancient Egypt was a civilized society, the government was able to organize the many thousands of workers needed to assemble the Pyramids. They were fed, clothed, and housed. Large-scale agriculture grew enough crops to feed the instant city that was created where the workers lived during the construction. The workers quarried the stones and cut them into precise blocks. They built ramps around the growing pyramid to cart heavy stones up to the level where they were working, and when they were finished they removed the ramps, leaving the pyramid.

The only reason the Egyptians were able to build a perfect pyramid was that they had been working on their pyramid-building skills for many hundreds of years already. The first pyramid-like structures were made of mud brick. They were called *mastabas*, and were short with flat tops. Next, an architect named Imhotep tried using stone to make a what looked like a stack of mastabas, one on top of another, to create a stepped pyramid known as Djoser's Pyramid, named after the king for whom it was built. Finally, the Egyptians tried to build a pyramid with straight sides. The engineers made some calculations and ordered the workers to lay their stones. After 10 feet, 15 feet, things still looked OK. As the pyramid rose higher and higher into the air, the engineers started to panic. Maybe the

angle was too steep! Maybe the pyramid would collapse, killing all the workers. They quickly stopped construction, redid their calculations, and gave orders for the building to begin again at a less steep angle. The pyramid was completed, and did not collapse, thanks to the correction in the slope of the sides! The engineers were ready to do a better job the next time, and by the time they built the Great Pyramid, the ancient Egyptians were experts.

Though the Pyramids never faded from view, many of the glories of ancient Egypt were largely forgotten while the rest of the world focused on rediscovering ancient Roman and Greek ruins and treasures. It was not until the French general Napoleon invaded Egypt in 1798 with almost 40,000 troops that the world became interested once again. Along with the soldiers, Napoleon brought with him an artist named Dominique Denon, who carefully sketched the numerous ruins the army encountered in their march through the Egyptian desert. The drawings were published in a book called *Voyage in Upper and Lower Egypt*, and later in a 24-volume set of books called *Description of Egypt*, and they stirred the world's imagination. What was life like in ancient Egypt? What other ruins were waiting to be discovered? Was there anything else hidden by the shifting sands of 4,000 years?

Before long, explorers and archaeologists had begun digging in Egypt. An Italian named Gio-

▲ *Excavations during the late 1800s at the Avenue of the Sphinxes.*

vanni Belzoni started work in 1817 and discovered several long-forgotten tombs. In 1822, the Egyptian Gallery opened at the recently built Louvre Museum in Paris. By 1850, excavation at the Avenue of the Sphinxes was started. A *sphinx* is a mythical creature that is half lion, half human, and the road was named for the more than 100 statues of sphinxes that lined the avenue. Long-buried tombs were rediscovered, some of them long empty because looters had robbed the graves hundreds of years earlier. Tourists flocked to

Egypt to see the Pyramids, and sometimes even climbed them, which is now outlawed. In 1880, William Flinders Petrie began work in Egypt. Petrie was one of the first archaeologists to make a serious effort to understand how the pyramids had been built, and he also studied how to sort different styles of pottery into groups, classify, and record them (as you will see in the activity later in this chapter). Egypt continued to reveal her secrets, year after year. Excavations continued through the 1890s and into the new century, and then came what seemed like the biggest find—the astonishing riches of King Tutankhamun discovered by Howard Carter in 1922.

Unbelievably, the amazing discoveries have not stopped. Maybe you have heard about a discovery made only a few years ago, when archaeologists in Bahariya, Egypt, stumbled onto an untouched burial ground containing 100 tombs full of jewelry, pottery, statues, and up to 10,000 mummies. This will surely keep archaeologists in Egypt busy for many years to come.

There are many clues that archaeologists use to tell if the remains they find at a site were once part of an ancient civilization. Some common remains of civilization are listed below:

- ◆ Evidence of writing (sometimes)
- ◆ Sculpture, painting, and decoration (usually)
- ◆ The wheel (sometimes)
- ◆ Large monuments or buildings (pyramids, temples, palaces, large statues)
- ◆ Advanced science, math, and engineering (a calendar, a pyramid, a sewer system, for example)
- ◆ Evidence of domesticated animals and agriculture (usually)
- ◆ Evidence of trade (artifacts that must have come from somewhere else)
- ◆ Using metal to make tools and artwork (sometimes)
- ◆ Evidence of a class system (rich people and poor people, leaders and common people)
- ◆ Evidence of territory (civilizations usually consist of a few large cities, not just one city, and need lots of land to grow crops—how many acres of wheat do you think it takes to feed 100,000 people?)

Not all of these things were part of each civilization, but all civilizations had at least four of them. The Neolithic period you read about in the last chapter was a time when some of the things listed were beginning to appear. How many of the checklist items could you find today, where you live? How do you think archaeologists can tell when they have found two cities that were part of the same civilization?

All civilizations began with trial and error as they experimented with science, math, and engineering. Archaeologists can look at an artifact or monument and tell roughly when it was made, based on the style and the technology that was used. Can you name ten inventions you think are still a little crude right now but will be improved upon in the future? What things do you have at home that already exist in a new, improved version?

▲ Art flourishes in civilizations. These Chinese roosters are about 2,000 years old.

Seriation *is a word that means putting things in a series, in date order. If you saw a kid walking down the street with his big brother, his mother, and his grandmother, you would be able to put them in order by age, even though you may not know their actual ages. Seriation is a method of relative dating where you know something is older than something else, but you don't know how much older. Archaeologists use seriation by looking at change in style and shape of something over time. One of the most common uses for seriation is in the study of Egyptian, Native American, and other ancient pottery. William Flinders Petrie (1853–1942) was one of the first archaeologists to use this method when he put ancient Egyptian pottery into date order by looking at the change in the style of pottery, but the real beauty of seriation is that it can be used for many things, including the kids down the street, and even cars. In order to be placed in a series, the items have to all be the same type of thing. That means you can't look at two kids and a dog and decide who is the oldest.*

In this game, look carefully at the six pictures labeled A–F. Based on style and shape, put the vehicles in order from oldest to most recent. Remember that with any invention, as years pass, improvements tend to be made. What are the differences between the oldest and the most recent vehicles? Which two cars are the most difficult to tell apart, and therefore the closest in age? How does the most recent car in the picture compare with a brand-new car you might see on the street?

How reliable is seriation? While seriation is usually a good way to place artifacts in date order, there are always exceptions. What if the kid down the street was really short for his age and his brother was very tall for his age? Sometimes cars can fool you as well. The Checker Cab Company made the same model of taxicab for more than 30 years, so you would be fooled if you tried to put their car into a series with other cars. Sometimes it takes a few years for one kind of technology or one design of pottery to be completely replaced by another. Look at the picture labeled G. It was taken about 1910. Even though the automobile had already been in use for more than 10 years by then, the people in the picture felt more comfortable using horses to pull the heavy boat to the launching site because horses still did a better job of pulling than the early automobile.

▲ *A*

▲ *B*

▼ C

◄ D

▲ F

▲ E

▲ G

The Sumerian and Babylonian Civilizations

◆ The ancient Egyptians weren't the only civilization in the world 5,000 years ago, but it wasn't until the 20th century that archaeologists found evidence of any other early civilizations. The first places early archaeologists looked for other civilizations were some of the places they

▲ *Austen Layard transported many large pieces from Babylonia, including this piece of the palace at Nimrud showing a ceremonial scene.*

had read about in the Bible. Babylonia, also known as Mesopotamia, the area along the Tigris and Euphrates Rivers in present-day southern Iraq, is mentioned many times in the Bible. In fact, it was the birthplace of Abraham, who became the Biblical founder of the Hebrew people after he traveled to Canaan.

The biblical people who lived in this region were called the Assyrians, and as early as the 1600s, adventurers brought back fragments of Assyrian artifacts they found there. These artifacts were about 3,000 years old. Strange, wedge-shaped writing called *cuneiform* had been found in the early 1800s, and was only deciphered after a man named Rawlinson found a text in three different languages on a cliff. This was similar to what had happened in Egypt with a rock called the Rosetta Stone, also written in three different languages and deciphered in the 19th century. It looked like the Assyrians had a true form of writing. As time passed, more and more exciting finds were made. Large British expeditions were sent into the area, called the Fertile Crescent because the ground was good for growing crops. By the mid-1800s, many large pieces of sculpture, even whole temples and walls filled with carvings, had been disassembled and brought back to the British Museum in England by a man named Austen H. Layard.

After a couple of unsuccessful attempts, he was able to send the colossal stone sculptures down the Tigris River on a raft, then by boat more than 2,000 miles all the way to London. Remains of large, steplike temple towers called *ziggurats* were also found during the 1800s. In the 1880s, the University of Pennsylvania in the United States sponsored an excavation at the ancient city of Nippur. Again, the treasures that were found were sent back to Pennsylvania to be studied and kept at the museum.

Archaeologists once again looked to the Bible for more inspiration, just as Heinrich Schliemann (whom you'll read about in the next chapter) looked to the stories of the ancient Greek poet Homer. Most people had heard the story of the Tower of Babel, when ancient Babylonians used baked mud bricks to build a high tower above everything else in the city. According to the story, God was unhappy with the Babylonians for thinking they could reach so high up in the sky, toward the heavens. Since one reason the people could do this was that they all spoke the same language, God caused them to speak many different languages and scattered them all across the world. The people were not able to continue building such a tower, because they could not understand each other.

Up until the late 1800s, people could not imagine what the Tower of Babel must have looked like. Most pictured it as a giant circular tower with a spiraling ramp reaching toward the top. Some people were not even sure it ever existed,

but in 1899 a German archaeologist named Robert Koldowey, excavating the city of Babylon, found the remains of a gigantic ziggurat 288 feet high and 288 feet wide, which required millions of mud bricks and must have taken hundreds of men years to construct. He had found the remains of the Tower of Babel.

◀ *This picture dates from 1694, and shows what people at the time thought the Tower of Babel looked like. Archaeologists have discovered that the Tower of Babel was probably a ziggurat, a kind of stepped pyramid common in Mesopotamia.*

Archaeologists looked at these remains from 1600 B.C.–600 B.C. and wondered how these people 3,000 years ago could have had such a complicated and developed system of writing, and could have had large cities and great temples. Maybe the Assyrians were not the first civilization in the area. Maybe there were others who came before, who invented the system of writing and started to build the great cities.

Beginning around the same time that Howard Carter was making the great discovery of King Tutankhamun's tomb in the Valley of Kings,

British archaeologist Sir Leonard Wooley (1880–1960) was hard at work along the Euphrates River, excavating deep into the ground. He chose the site of the city of Ur, mentioned in the Bible as the birthplace of Abraham. His hundreds of workmen dug more than 35 feet down, where they came upon the remains of the "lost" civilization people had been wondering about, buried for more than 5,000 years.

The spectacular finds included the Royal Tombs, dating to about 2700 B.C. with a total of more than 2,000 graves, including 16 royal

Money Matters

Archaeologists have found money made from shells, stone, and metal at sites around the world. Trade was one of the most important aspects of early civilization. Writing developed as an easier way of keeping track of traded and sold goods; in fact, the first examples of writing in the world are Sumerian bills and documents dealing with grain and other bought and sold items. Money was invented so people could have a standard measure of value; however, one group of people would

sometimes introduce their money into the places they traveled or invaded. You can imagine the confusion when different people with different money wanted to buy things from each other.

Imagine you are an ancient trader. You have come to town with your shell money and a cow you have just bought for 20 shells. Now you meet a man from a faraway town who has a goat that cost him 10 stone rings. You are not sure how much a stone ring is worth, but you think you can

figure it out because you know that a cow is worth four goats. If the stranger wants to buy your cow, how many pieces of stone money should he give you? Here's a hint: In order to solve this problem, you need to figure out how much four goats, the equivalent of one cow, would cost stone money.

ANSWER: 40 stone rings.

graves. There was a king and queen buried at Ur, along with many servants and attendants and animals, who had been sacrificed to accompany them to the afterlife. The skeletons lay in a pattern, each one just where the body had fallen, all part of an elaborate religious ceremony. In addition to the human remains, the Royal Tombs were filled with vessels of gold, silver, and a soft, semi-transparent stone called calcite, and beautiful jewelry made of gold, lapis lazuli, and carnelian, a fiery red stone in the quartz family.

The queen, whose name was Puabi, was buried with a golden headdress lined with beautiful colored stones, and a cape studded with more than 100 strings of gold, silver, lapis, carnelian, and agate beads (agate is another colorful stone in the quartz family). Puabi also wore a large necklace and 10 golden rings on her fingers. The king was buried with one of the oldest musical instruments ever found, the "Great Lyre," more than 5 feet wide and 5 feet high, with an expertly shaped gold sculpture of a bull's head on the front. The bull was a special beast in Sumerian culture. Some of the metal bowls and containers found at Ur have the mark of a bull's leg on them. Without more clues, though, it will be hard for anyone today to understand exactly what the bull meant to Sumerians and why it was so special.

Around the same time that Wooley was excavating at Ur, German archaeologists were able to go even further back in time. They excavated extensively at Uruk, known in Biblical times as the city of Erech. There, they found the earliest remains of the Sumerian civilization, dating back to about 3500 B.C. In the layers of dirt below, they then found evidence of a Neolithic culture called the Ubaid that existed there from 4200 B.C. The Ubaid were a culture who built ceremonial temples and farmed and herded animals. As time passed, their settlements got bigger and bigger. They expanded across Mesopotamia and traded with the people at the edges of their civilization. As the Ubaid became more powerful and prosperous, they built bigger temples.

What else have archaeologists learned about Sumerians? Archaeologists working with these artifacts looked at all the lapis lazuli, carnelian, and other gemstones that were found, and realized that the Sumerians must have traded with people in what is now Pakistan and India for these gems, since there was no natural source nearby. Even gold and silver were brought in from places as far away as Turkey. The evidence that trade was important also showed up as archaeologists translated the cuneiform writing on the cylinder seals and clay tablets they had found. Many of the earliest writings were records of sales and trades, and it seems that writing was first developed as a way to keep track of sales information. In fact, the Neolithic people who preceded the Sumerians used clay tokens in hollow clay balls as a way to keep track of sales and exchanges.

The Sumerians were also the first civilization to invent the wheel and to use the arch in their construction. They had an advanced understanding of science and mathematics. As archaeologists discovered, the ancient Greeks and Romans borrowed many of their ideas for their own use, beginning when Alexander the Great conquered Mesopotamia 2,400 years ago. Many of our engineering and mathematical ideas are with us today courtesy of the brilliant Sumerians, the forgotten ancient civilization that Wooley rediscovered.

◇◇◇◇◇◇◇◇◇◇◇◇◇◇◇◇◇◇◇◇◇◇◇◇◇

Cultural Treasures

Back in the early 19th century, Belzoni and Layard sent many priceless treasures back to Europe. Even during the early 20th century, it was still common for expeditions to be sponsored by major universities, which in turn wound up with most of the artifacts in their own museums. The popular Indiana Jones *movies feature Harrison Ford as a 1930s professor whose university sends him in search of various one-of-a-kind treasures to be displayed in its museum.*

These days, the removal of large-scale artifacts and buildings from their original countries has stopped because people realize it is not right to take the ancient treasures away from their original context, and that they rightfully belong to the descendants of the people who made and built them. Some especially valuable or meaningful artifacts have been returned to their original countries, and now many newly found ancient sites are being excavated and left where they are so tourists and scientists can learn as much as possible about these early civilizations.

Of course, if every artifact stayed exactly where it was found, museums would not be able to teach us anything about other cultures. The most popular idea is for museums to send their collections on a "world tour" so everyone has a chance to see them. This happened during the late 20th century when the treasures of King Tutankhamun sold millions of tickets on a tour of the United States. Those universities that were able to get treasures from other countries also share them; the University of Pennsylvania's tomb treasures from Ur were on display in New York City recently.

Many civilizations came up with a system of writing, invented the wheel, and figured out how to build large monuments. Some people wondered if these early people got their ideas from elsewhere. After all, somebody had to come up with the idea first, right?

Archaeologists know that independent invention happened all over the world. That is, people who had never met came up with the same ideas and solutions to complicated problems. Independent invention continues to happen even today. It happened with the invention of the automobile—scientists in different countries were all experimenting with the same ideas at the same time. You can test this idea with a friend using some pencils and a few pounds of clay. Try to make a pencil holder that can hold several pencils. Tell your friend to do the same thing in another room.

What did you come up with? What did your friend come up with? Was it a cup-type holder, or maybe a large ball where you stick the pencils directly into the clay like a giant pincushion? You and your friend will likely both make something that looks the same because there is only one good answer to the problem. The pincushion idea might work, but it might leave clay remnants on the point of the pencil, and it won't work so well for unsharpened pencils. If you think about it, there are many problems that have only one basic solution, and people around the world are smart enough to think of it on their own.

Sometimes people used what they found with little or even no modifications. In ancient Sumerian society, for example, women found that one half of a cockle shell made an excellent container for the many different colors of makeup they owned. Because this is not a complicated idea, people in other places who use makeup and have access to shells could easily come up with the very same idea on their own.

Writing is another independent invention. Go to the library and look at foreign language dictionaries for French, Spanish, German, Japanese, and Hebrew. If you have friends from other countries, ask them to write out the alphabets of their native countries. How do other alphabets compare to ours? Which ones are closest and which are the least similar? The ones that are closest probably developed from the same root alphabet, while the ones that are most different from each other prob-ably developed independently. Some alphabets, such as the Chinese alphabet, are pretty close to the way they were when invented thousands of years ago!

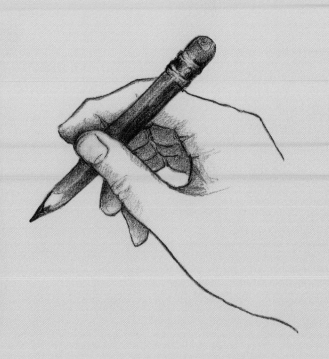

Chinese Civilization—
The Shang Dynasty

◆ While artifacts are often very similar from one civilization to the next, sometimes there are unique designs or technologies that can help

The three-footed vessel is one unique characteristic of the Shang Dynasty civilization in China. ▶

archaeologists identify exactly where something came from and how old it is. In China, by 1700 B.C., a civilization had developed that is called the Shang Dynasty culture. They had writing, the wheel, and large burial complexes like other civilizations, but when the Shang civilization was excavated, beginning during the 1920s, archaeologists discovered many artifacts that are not found anywhere else. These include:

Oracle bones These were bones from oxen, or sometimes sections of tortoise shell, with a question for the gods inscribed on them. Hot metal was pressed against the bone, and then a special "fortune-teller" would read the cracks made by the heat and announce an answer.

Tripod vessels People of the Shang Dynasty used many different styles of clay containers, including three-footed vessels that are rarely found elsewhere in the world. Have you ever seen a three-legged container before?

Lost wax vessels The Shang Dynasty people knew how to use bronze. They had an ingenious method for making beautiful, intricately designed bronze objects. They would take a large block of wax and carve whatever design they wanted into it. Since wax is soft and carves well, it was easy to do very detailed work. Next, they covered the carved wax completely with

Pottery Classification

Pottery is one of the most common items found at the site of an ancient civilization. When pots and jars are found as part of a burial, chances are better they will be in one piece. Grouping similar pots and jars together is called classification. *This helps archaeologists figure out which shapes and patterns were most popular, and also makes seriation possible. At many sites, so much pottery is found that classification of each piece can take many weeks or even months. Petrie, the archaeologist mentioned earlier in this chapter, was one of the pioneers of classification.*

MATERIALS
◆ *Paper*
◆ *Pencil or pen*

Look at the drawings below. Can you group these containers into seven different types based on shape? Now start again, but group them into five types by their design or pattern.

ANSWERS: Five types, by pattern: (1) A, F, and I, (2) C and L, (3) E and K, (4) J, H, and K, (5) B and D; Seven types, by shape: (1) D and G (2) J and L, (3) K and H, (4) E, F, and B, (5) A, (6) C, (7) I

clay and heated it until the wax melted away. Then they poured molten bronze into the clay cast. When the bronze hardened and cooled, they could crack away the clay, leaving the beau- tiful bronze object. Today, jewelry is sometimes made using this "lost wax" casting technique.

Build Your Own Screen

MATERIALS

- ◆ *Scissors*
- ◆ *Sturdy rectangular cardboard box, about 12 inches wide x 16 inches long x 4 inches high, or two thin pieces of wood that are 4 x 12 inches and two that are 4 x 16 inches*
- ◆ *Stapler*
- ◆ *Section of mesh screen, not too fine—at least ⅛ inch mesh (you can find it at a home improvement or hardware store)*
- ◆ *Newspaper (if you are using wood to make the screen)*
- ◆ *Heavy-duty glue (if you are using wood to make the screen)*
- ◆ *Drawer handles (from a home improvement or hardware store)*

Cut the bottom out of the box with scissors, leaving only the four sides. Have an adult staple the screen around the edges of the box. If you are using wood, lay down the newspaper and use the glue to attach the pieces so you have a rectangle. Let it dry according to the instructions on the glue container. Now have an adult staple the screen around the bottom edges.

You can attach a drawer handle to each of the shorter sides of the screen by either gluing it or screwing it in. If you are trying to screw it in, get an adult to drill the holes for you first.

Now you have a screen.

Get a friend to shovel some dirt into the screen as you shake it back and forth. Hold it away from you so you don't get your sneakers covered in dirt. What is left in your screen after you shake it well? Do you see anything that could be an artifact?

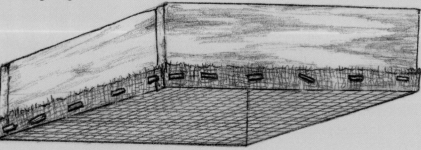

The End of Civilization?

◆ The civilizations mentioned earlier all peaked between 4,000 and 2,000 years ago. What happened after that? Did the people in Egypt, Mesopotamia, and China go back to living in Neolithic villages? Archaeologists continue to uncover remains not only from when these great civilizations were at their height, but also after they began to decline. The ability of archaeologists to keep excavating today depends on the political situation in the places they want to work. For example, bombing during the Persian Gulf War may have damaged some Babylonian sites, and tensions between Iraq and the United States and its allies may limit access to others.

In Egypt, the power of the pharaohs faded and other people controlled Egypt, including the Persians, the Nubians from the region south of Egypt, the Greeks, and the Romans. One of the greatest cities in the ancient world was Alexandria, built in Egypt in honor of Alexander the Great, the Greek general who had arrived there in 332 B.C. Later, during the Roman, or Coptic, period, Egypt was introduced to Christianity. Artifacts from this time show a mixture of classical Egyptian designs with Roman and Greek ideas, and Christian images such as the crucifix. Although archaeologists have found some spectacular art from these later periods, especially

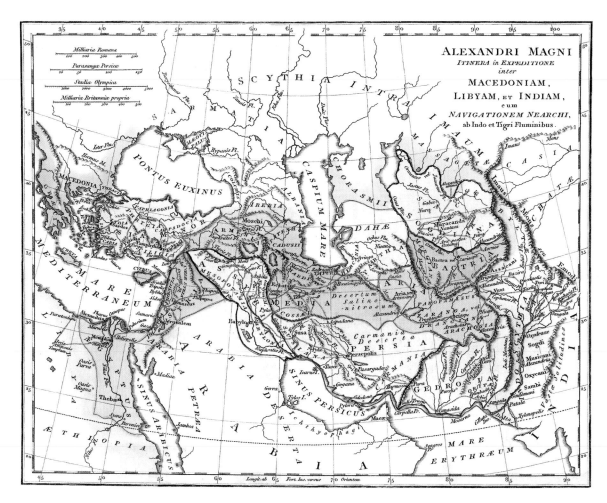

▲ *Alexander the Great conquered Egypt and Mesopotamia more than 2,000 years ago. On this 1807 map showing Alexander's conquests, Egypt is written in Latin as Aegyptus.*

painted onto wooden coffins, Egypt could never again match the feat of the pyramids.

In Mesopotamia, there were many other cultures after the Sumerians, including the mighty

Assyrians. Eventually, many other peoples invaded—the Greeks, Romans, Arabs, and Turks all took turns ruling the territory—and over the years the great civilization declined until there was nothing left above ground but a few ruins.

In China, other great powerful dynasties followed the Shang Dynasty. In 1974, peasants found the remains of the Mausoleum of Shi Huangdi, where a Qin Dynasty emperor was buried with 7,000 life-sized terra cotta soldiers in the late 3rd century B.C. You have also heard of the 4,000-mile-long Great Wall of China, started during the Han Dynasty in the 3rd century B.C. to keep out invaders, but ironically destroyed by fighting and neglect within China over the next several hundred years. It was not until the Ming Dynasty, also famous for its valuable vases, that the wall was rebuilt in its present form. Political division, infighting, and Mongol invasions made it hard for the Chinese to match the accomplishments of the great Shang era.

Do you think archaeologists in the distant future will excavate the late 20th and early 21st centuries and believe that we were a great civilization? Have we peaked already, are we at our peak now, or will our civilization peak in the future? What artifacts from today might impress an archaeologist of the future most?

The early civilizations of Asia were not the only civilizations in the ancient world. In fact, as the glory of these first civilizations was fading, a new civilization was coming into existence. Greek civilization began to blossom toward the beginning of the last millennium B.C., and before long, Alexander the Great was conquering Egypt and Babylonia. The Greeks, along with the Romans, who came into power not long after the Greeks, had vast empires stretching across many hundreds of miles. Many of their ideas and innovations are still with us today, as you will see in the next chapter.

Sometimes, old legends can hide the truth about a civilization. According to the Old Testament, King Solomon's men returned from a foreign place by the sea called Ophir with 25,000 pounds of gold and other precious items. Hundreds of years after this was supposed to have taken place, travelers to southeast Africa wrote about the riches of the gold mines. People began to believe this place must be the location of the biblical "King Solomon's Mines," as they now called them. In the 1870s, a German explorer named Karl Mauch located a huge stone enclosure measuring 750 feet around with a 30-foot high tower atop a hill. He remembered the story of Solomon's gold, and thought this building was somehow connected to the legend, built 2,000 years before by Solomon's men.

The discovery created a stir among adventurers and fortune seekers, who then proceeded to ransack the ruins looking for treasure. A writer named H. Ryder Haggard wrote a book called *King Solomon's Mines* in 1885, and it made people even more curious. Between 1892 and 1894, gold hunters looted the site at will. Not long after that, a private company got permission to take what they wanted from many African ruins, and they came away with 30 pounds of gold.

Finally, laws were passed to protect African ruins, and serious archaeology could begin. In the end, archaeologists found that the site, known as the Great Zimbabwe, was begun by an African civilization more than 700 years ago. They were technologically advanced, and were able to build the structure with tightly fitted stones, using no mor-

The Great Enclosure at the Great Zimbabwe. ▶

tar. The people lived in thatched huts in a city of between 10,000 and 20,000 people and traded their gold, and ivory from the tusks of elephants, for cloth and ceramic from places as far away as Asia.

Today, the Great Zimbabwe is open to the public, who can wander around the ruins and gaze in wonder at the ingenuity of this ancient African civilization.

◀ *Narrow passageway inside the complex at the Great Zimbabwe. Archaeologists have proved the site was an ancient African city, not King Solomon's mines.*

5 Greece and Rome

The ashes in many places were already knee-deep; and the boiling showers which came from the steaming breath of the volcano forced their way into the houses, bearing with them a strong and suffocating vapor. In some places, immense fragments of rock, hurled upon the house roofs, bore down the street along with masses of confused ruin . . . cinder and rock lay matted in heaps, from beneath which emerged the half-hid limbs of some crushed and mangled fugitive . . . Bright and gigantic through the darkness . . . the mountain [Vesuvius] shone—a pile of fire! Another—and another—

and another—shower of ashes, far more profuse than before, scattered fresh desolation on the streets.

—Sir Edward Bulwer, *The Last Days of Pompeii*, 1834

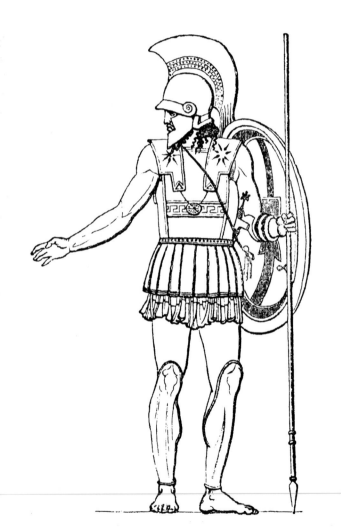

You emerge from the colorfully tiled bath, dry off, and then use and flush the toilet. You rinse your hands, and go to the bedroom. Before you get into bed, you make a neat stack of the coins by your bed, and take a little sip of wine from a small bottle. You apply some ointment to a bug bite on your face, put on a little perfume, and then turn out the light and go to sleep.

What year is it? Where are you? Is it this year somewhere in America?

Would you believe it is the year A.D. 200 in an ancient Roman villa?

The ancient Romans and Greeks ate many of the same foods we do and had many of the same rituals and luxuries we have today. The wealthiest Romans had flush toilets and baths in their homes. They wore jewelry and had a coin-based system of money. Their architecture, sculpture, and design was beautiful and famous in its own time; but then it was mostly forgotten for several hundred years. Even the famous Colosseum, where the movie *Gladiator* was set, fell into ruin. Then, in the 15th and 16th centuries, Classical Roman and Greek culture was rediscovered during the time called the Renaissance, from the French word for "rebirth." Renaissance statues like Michaelangelo's *David* are world famous.

One reason the Roman and Greek worlds were fascinating was the size of their empires and the ambition of their builders. Some of the greatest engineers in the ancient world were Romans and Greeks. The Greeks built large, open-air amphitheaters out of stone and the Romans copied this idea. The Romans also built aqueducts to carry water from the mountains to their towns and cities, and built bridges of stone. Everywhere they went, they left their mark on the countryside, and thousands of years later, the remains of their engineering marvels are still standing. From Britain to Germany to Israel to Syria, and all the way to Egypt, Roman and Greek ruins are common sights.

Centuries after the Renaissance, the popular Neoclassical ("new classical") style was another revival of the Greek and Roman design. Even into the 21st century, new buildings are being built in the classical style. Chances are, wherever you live, you can find a building with classical features. Maybe the front porch of your own house, or maybe your local bank or post office, has Greek-style columns. Maybe there is a Roman- or Greek-style statue in a nearby park or town square. This eternal presence of the classical culture in our everyday lives may be why archaeologists have always been fascinated with finding the buried remains of the ancient Greeks and Romans.

The first real discoveries of the "lost" Roman era were the forgotten cities of Pompeii and Herculaneum, buried under 50 feet of ash and mud by the spectacular eruption of Mount Vesuvius in A.D. 79. Pompeii was almost rediscovered in the late 1500s, but the marble fragments found at that time were not recognized for what they were. More than 100 years later, after the accidental discovery of this ancient marble, many fabulous treasures were extracted by a wealthy Austrian prince for use on his own estate and gardens. It would still be more than 50 years before any truly systematic excavations took place. Little by little, since the 1760s, parts of the ancient city have been completely dug out so today's tourists can enjoy Pompeii as it appeared just before that fateful eruption. Many villas and homes were well preserved, including wine jugs, wall paintings, and beautiful mosaic tile floors. Even after 250 years, there are still sections of the city that have not yet been excavated!

People in the 1700s and 1800s were fascinated by the buildings, artwork, and artifacts that were discovered. Almost every imaginable item of daily life had been found at Pompeii and Herculaneum. Pots of food were still on the hearths, and bread still in ovens. Can you imagine how carefully archaeologists had to excavate to preserve the context of all the artifacts?

Lava and ash had even hardened around people who were trapped in the city at the time of the eruption. After a while, their bodies disintegrated, leaving cavities in a shell of hardened lava the shape of the person. In the mid-1800s, it was discovered that by pouring plaster into the molds and letting it harden, archaeologists could bring back life-sized casts of Pompeian citizens as they tried to escape death. Drawings were printed and many books were written on the subject, including the book quoted at the beginning of the chapter. Once in a while, some of the treasures of Pompeii and Herculaneum make a tour of different museums around the world. If you ever have the chance to see them, don't miss it!

The Lost City of Troy

◆ The Greek civilization also had many fans and enthusiasts. Heinrich Schliemann was a successful German businessman who taught himself to speak 16 languages and retired in 1863 at the age of 41 to pursue his dream of finding the lost city of Troy. He had read the epic story called *The Iliad*, by Homer, and knew all about the siege of the city of Troy, including how the Greek soldiers hid in a giant wooden horse and surprised the Trojans. Schliemann also knew about all the

▲ *Thousands of well-preserved artifacts were uncovered at Pompeii, including these amphorae, storage containers for wine.*

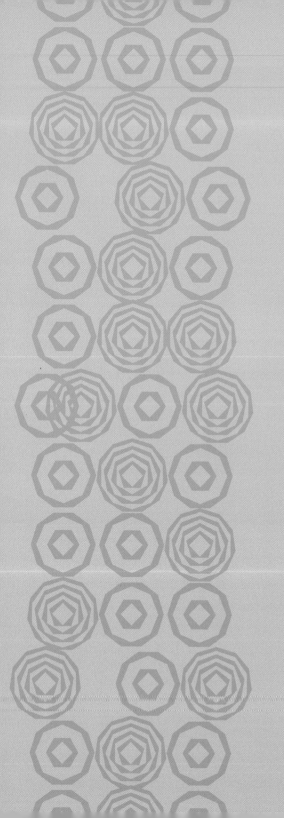

Stratigraphy is the natural or artificial layering of the ground. The idea of stratigraphy is that the further down into the ground you go, the farther back in time you are going. As Heinrich Schliemann discovered, stratigraphy can be very helpful in separating and dating the artifacts from different occupations at the same site. If you go outside and dig a hole three feet deep, you will most likely notice a change in the color and the way it feels in your hand—gritty, dry, claylike, etc.—at least once, but probably a few times.

MATERIALS

◆ *Small shovel*

◆ *Ruler*

◆ *Pad of paper*

◆ *Pencil*

First, get permission to dig outside. Start with a hole that is at least four inches wide. Dig the hole as deep as you can, but at least eight inches deep, if possible. Now look at the cross section (view from the side) of soil you just revealed. Going by the color of the soil, see if you can identify different layers in the soil. Using your ruler, measure the thickness of each distinct layer of earth, writing down the color and texture. Archaeologists use a standard chart that was developed many years ago, called the Munsell Color Chart, so they have a uniform system for referring to soil colors all over the world. How many different layers did you find in your little excavation?

As you learned in Chapter 2, decaying twigs, leaves, and animal remains make up the top layer of soil, or humus. Over the years, new soil is made with the help of earthworms, and deposited over the older soil. New plants grow in the humus, which is also known as topsoil, for reasons you can imagine. As you go further down into the ground, you are reaching soil that has lost some of its organic (plant and animal) nutrients. You won't find the rich black or dark chocolate brown color anymore. The dirt will get lighter. If you keep going, you may find more rocks, or you may find a tan-colored, more sandy soil. Depending on where you live, this could be a deposit from a retreating glacier about 10,000 years ago during the last Ice Age. Glaciers moved large and small rocks, rounding and polishing them by grinding them slowly over thousands of years. If you live in a place the glaciers did not reach during the Ice Age, it is possible polished and rounded stones you find were created by the waves of an ancient ocean or lake.

All of these things are part of natural stratigraphy. When you are working at an archaeological site, you can separate the different layers by the changing soil color and texture. Sometimes other events help create stratigraphy. The Great Fire in New York in the 19th century left behind a charred layer over many blocks of the city that helps archaeologists know when they have hit the year 1835. When archaeologists like Schliemann excavate places where there have been many occupations at the same site, the stratigraphy can help tell them how much time passed between occupations. If there are several layers of dirt between two cities on the same site, archaeologists can guess that some time passed between when the first city was lived in and when the second city was occupied. On the other hand, if the archaeologists find a layer of silt, they can imagine a flood ended the occupation of the first city, and then people built a new city on top.

—— *Rich black soil (fine)*

—— *Dark chocolate soil (fine)*

—— *Milk chocolate soil (rocky)*

—— *Gray/brown soil (coarse)*

—— *Pale mustard soil (rocky)*

—— *Sandy Soil (fire)*

riches described in the book, including the bars of solid gold, elaborate suits of armor, and shiploads of treasure. This wonderful city had to be real; it was described in so much detail. But where could it be? After preparing himself for five years, with his copy of *The Iliad* in hand, Schliemann found a site in northwest Turkey he thought would be the best place to excavate, a huge mound called Hissarlik.

▼ A tomb at Mycenae.

After three years of digging, Schliemann and his workers uncovered the remains of not one, but seven occupations on the same site, one on top of the other. It was unclear at first which layer was the Troy of Homer's time, until Schliemann found that the second level from the bottom contained the most impressive remains, including gold and jewels he called "Priam's Treasure." It turned out his conclusion was wrong. Other dating methods proved this level dated to before 2200 B.C., while today, archaeologists believe the mythical Troy of *The Iliad* was really much closer to the top of the mound. Even though Schliemann was wrong about which level was the Troy of legend, he had discovered the importance of *stratigraphy*, or the layering of different types of soil in the ground.

Schliemann was allowed to continue his excavation in another part of the Aegean, this time at Mycenae in Greece. He still had *The Iliad* close by, because Mycenae was supposed to be the home of the ancient house of Atreus, a royal family that led the forces to the city of Troy. After years of work, Schliemann discovered several shaft graves, including one he thought was the grave of the mythical king Agamemnon. In it, he found the remains of a bearded man who crumbled to dust after Schliemann removed the fantastic gold death mask covering the king's face. He later discovered the mask was too old to be from Agamemnon's time.

Underwater Archaeology

◆ The Romans had a large empire that stretched from the British Isles all the way to northern Africa and western Asia. The fastest way to get people and supplies across vast distances was by boat. The Mediterranean Sea was a great way to reach most of the Roman Empire, and many fine ports were built by the Romans along the Mediterranean. Everything, from wine and glassware to coins and gold bars, was shipped via the sea.

Both Romans and Greeks had fine ships and smaller sailing craft built to speed along the sea, usually with the help of slaves who rowed and rowed until they could no longer move their arms. Still, these fine ships were no match for the fierce thunderstorms that occasionally struck. They were also easy prey for pirates, and were sometimes sunk by enemy vessels during times of war. The sunken ships found a home at the bottom of the Mediterranean Sea and the mouth of the Atlantic Ocean, as deep as 2,000 feet below the surface.

The first time underwater archaeology was attempted, in 1775, the early divers had trouble getting through the silt and mud covering the artifacts on the bed of the Tiber River in Italy. It took more than 100 years for real interest to develop in underwater archaeology. As you read

▲ *A Greek boat. Sturdy as they were, many Greek and Roman vessels sank in violent weather—along with whatever cargo they were carrying.*

in Chapter 1, there are many steps to go through while doing archaeology. Now imagine how much more difficult it might be to run an underwater archaeology expedition! First, you need archaeologists who also know how to dive and are not afraid of spending long periods of time in the cold, murky water. Unless the shipwreck is just offshore, you will need a large boat to serve as your command center, a place where divers can jump in from and bring artifacts back to, and rest while other divers go underwater. Of course, before you start, you have to be even more sure of where your site is located. It costs money to rent a boat and get supplies like oxygen for the divers, so you wouldn't want to waste your time unless you were pretty sure of the location of a

Underwater Archaeology Game

As you have read, it is very difficult for underwater archaeologists to do their jobs. Mapping and recording the artifacts they find, and then bringing them to the surface, can be a real challenge. In this game you will try to perform these difficult tasks yourself.

MATERIALS
◆ *Bucket or old washtub, ²/₃ full of lukewarm water*
◆ *Pad of plain white paper*
◆ *Pen and pencil*
◆ *5 paper clips, different sizes*
◆ *3 small pebbles*
◆ *Eraser, about 2 inches long*
◆ *Ceramic coffee mug*
◆ *Stainless steel fork and spoon*
◆ *Handful of pennies*
◆ *String*
◆ *Sand or soil*
◆ *Short-sleeved shirt (you will need to wear this!)*

Place the coffee mug slowly at the bottom of the bucket, and then, starting with the paper clip and ending with the pennies, drop in the rest of the items near the mug. First, try to sketch how the items look, noting their positions. Can you see where everything is? Now add the sand or soil and allow it to settle. What can you see now?

Next, tie string to one of the paper clips and pull it up to the surface slowly, without it falling back into the water. Try the same method for the eraser, and then the ceramic mug, without disturbing the context of the other "artifacts." It is not so easy, is it? Archaeologists who work underwater have limited time, so if they want to get at certain interesting artifacts it is not always easy to do it without disturbing other artifacts.

shipwreck. After all this, once your divers are underwater, doing real archaeology can be very difficult.

In the 1950s, the famous French explorer Jacques Cousteau found the remains of a Roman galley and brought back many treasures from the wreck. Some people thought it was unfortunate that he hadn't noted the context or location of any of the artifacts. Imagine you are diving and you have found an *amphora*, a container widely used during Roman times, poking out from the sea floor, partly covered with coral. It may be hard enough to remove the vessel from the mud, never mind noting the position of the artifact and possibly using an underwater camera to take a picture. In many underwater locations, when you try to step on the sea floor, the dirt and sediment is kicked up, creating a cloud of dust so you can't see much of anything. You have to be patient, yet time is short because of your limited oxygen supply.

Over the centuries, storms have stirred up the sea floor, especially where the ships are in more shallow water. Even though there are often written accounts or maps showing where ships sank, sometimes wrecks have shifted so far from where they sank that archaeologists cannot find them; and just as on dry land, there is a chance looters have been to the site first and carelessly taken what they could, breaking and destroying the rest of the treasures in the process.

Even though it is difficult, the lure of finding well-preserved treasures, untouched for nearly 2,000 years, keeps underwater archaeology alive. The number of ships sunk since ancient times is well into the thousands, and only a fraction of the wrecks have ever been found. But underwater archaeology can be dangerous. In the case of the *Titanic*, the wreck is so far under the surface of the ocean that only a remote-controlled robot could make the trip down. In most cases, the archaeologists can only bring a portion of the treasures to the surface. Even if they have survived, the actual remains of the ship are almost never brought up, because of their weight and size. After so many years underwater, most wooden vessels would crumble to dust after being brought to the surface. So what do underwater archaeologists bring to the surface? Most of the time, their finds consist of bronze and silver coins, amphorae and other smaller containers, plates, oil lamps, and statues. Many of these treasures wind up in museums all around the world.

A newspaper from the 1830s describes shipwrecks of the time. How many can you count? ▶

THE SUN.

From the Halifax Gazette, of May 21.

Our paper of to-day contains melancholy accounts of shipwrecks and the loss of human life. We saw a person yesterday who was at Louisburg when the Astrea was lost. The survivors had reached that place. They informed him that that vessel struck on the morning of the 7th instant, against some high cliffs at Little Lorain Head, about five miles from Louisburg and almost instantaneously went to pieces: that she had studding sails set at the time, and up to the fatal moment of striking had been going at the rate of ten knots. The only individuals saved were the surgeon, carpenter, and one seaman, who were thrown almost insensible on some of the cliffs.

SYDNEY, May 14.—Barque Astrea, William Ridley, master, with *two hundred and eleven passengers* and crew, went ashore at Loren, near Louisburg, morning of the 7th inst., and only the surgeon and two of the crew saved! Same day, brig Edward struck a piece of ice near Port Nova, and sunk immediately—crew saved. On the 10th, brig Fidelity, Clarke, from Dublin, for Quebec, went ashore on Scattari and was lost; passengers and crew, 150 in number, saved. Same day, brig Columbus, Russell, from Newcastle for Quebec, was lost three miles east of Louisburg, crew saved. On the 27th ult. lat 45 20, lon 48 53, the Margaret, Walsh, from Newcastle, picked up the captain of barque James, from Ireland for Quebec, with ten others, only survivors of two hundred and sixty-five persons on board the James when she sprung aleak and sunk.

The crew of barque Charlotte Langin, of New Brunswick, from Liverpool for Philadelphia has been landed here from an American fishing vessel. The ship had sprung aleak and they had abandoned her. They were three days in their boats.

Ship Marchioness of Queensbury, from Liverpool for Miramachi, went ashore on Cape Tormentine, night of 16th inst., but will be got off if the weather continues moderate.

Three vessels bound to Quebec with passengers, (one of them, the Jane, of Workington,) are reported ashore on St. Paul's.

Barque John Atkins, from Halifax for Richmond went ashore three miles from that place, and was totally lost.

On the night of the 15th inst. brig Margaret, from Belfast for St. Johns, N. B. went ashore at Barrington, and was totally lost—crew saved. The mate's wife and four children were drowned.

☞ TO PAINTERS.—At a meeting of P

Conquering distant lands and fighting off invasions were important in Greek and Roman society, so of course there were many ancient battles. The Peloponnesian War in Greece was a 30-year long struggle between the city-states of Athens and Sparta. Excavations in downtown Athens in 1997 uncovered several polyandreia, *or communal burials, holding cremated remains which might have been soldiers of the Greek leader, Pericles.*

Once the Greek archaeologists examined all the pottery fragments and other artifacts in the graves, they sent the bone remains to a physical anthropologist named Anagnosti Agelarakis, who has been working to identify who the bones belonged to, their health, their diet, how old they were when they died, and their physical characteristics.

Though archaeologists are often the ones who find ancient bones, physical anthropologists are specially trained to examine bones. The first step is sorting, classifying, and measuring the bone fragments. Then, examination with the naked eye and possibly microscope is done, and finally, chemical testing can show the make-up of the bones and answer many other questions.

Greek and Roman Life

◆ As you saw on the first page of this chapter, life in Greek and Roman civilization was similar to modern life in many ways. It is thanks to archaeological exploration of "lost" cities such as Troy, Pompeii, and Herculaneum that we know a great deal about Greek and Roman life. While there are pictures and descriptions from ancient times still in existence, archaeologists have found actual remains to prove what the Greeks and Romans ate and how they dressed. We know that they ate bread, apples, grapes, figs, olives, meat, and fish, and also that they used many herbs and spices, partly because archaeologists have found remains of these foods. We know what kind of clothes they wore and how their soldiers dressed because buckles, pins, parts of sandals, and jewelry turn up at excavations. Pictures and faded paintings can never do justice to the actual artifacts, some of them restored to their original glory and others found in perfect condition after being buried under ash and hardened mud for almost 2,000 years.

Archaeologists working in Egypt and Mesopotamia have found that many Greek and Roman inventions really originated in those even older civilizations. The famous arch of Roman bridges and aqueducts was originally invented by the Sumerians more than 2,000 years earlier; but, because the few surviving Sumerian examples are in faraway and sometimes desolate places, while there are many surviving Roman examples all over Europe, we tend to think of the Romans as the inventors of the arch.

There were many scientists, mathematicians, and inventors among the Greeks and Romans. If you have not yet heard of Pythagoras, you will come across him when you study geometry in math class. How about Pliny, who studied the eruption of Mount Vesuvius in A.D. 79? Or how about Herodotus, who observed an Egyptian mummy being prepared and wrapped and wrote about it? There were also many philosophers and political commentators. Maybe you have heard of Socrates, Plato, and Aristotle? There were also plenty of poets and playwrights, such as Homer, Euripides, Sophocles, and Aristophanes. As you saw earlier, sometimes their plays or epic poems can be used to help archaeologists find lost treasures or see if certain legends were based on true stories.

Poetry and other writings were read in special places invented by the Romans called *auditoriums*, or places to hear. Theater was also a very important part of Greek and Roman life. The Greeks started out with small theaters with wooden stages, but when one collapsed in 500 B.C., they decided to use stone. By using the natural slope of a hillside, the Greeks, and then the Romans, could build the seats of their theaters easily, without any supports. Bleachers—the kind you might see at a high school football or soccer game—have metal supports holding them together, so each row is higher than the next and everybody can see the action on the field.

Once the Romans were expert at building this kind of theater, they built the first stone theater in Rome itself, which held more than 50,000 people. Just 125 years later, in A.D. 80, construction was finished on the monstrous Colosseum. Built on a six-acre site to hold up to 87,000 people, the ruins of this engineering marvel still stand in downtown Rome. Thousands of people and animals died in the ring while fighting before throngs of cheering fans. When the Emperor was in attendance, he would signal with his thumb whether he thought the contestant should live or die.

Besides violent sports, the Romans loved other, less bloody, kinds of activities. They built the gigantic Circus Maximus, which by some estimates could hold as many as 300,000 people. It had an oval track, and it was where the Romans held chariot races (two or four horses pulling a carriage around seven times) and mock fights taking place on horseback. Both Romans and Greeks idealized the human body. The Greeks thought of exercise as one of the most important parts of a child's education. Gymnasiums were special places where Greek children would go to exercise and play games. Sound familiar? The

▲ *Greeks and Romans built their theaters on hillsides so spectators could easily see the stage. This picture shows the remains of the Greek theater at Delphi.*

most common sports were tug-of-war, ball games, running, jumping, boxing, and wrestling. The Greeks loved sports so much, they invented the original Olympics as a way to bring people together from all parts of the country to compete.

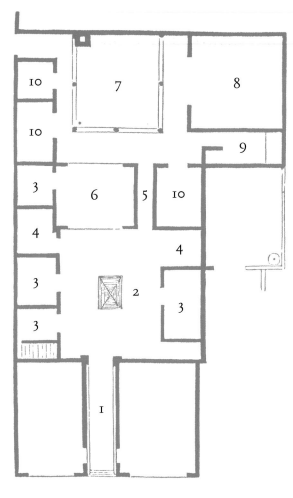

▲ *Floor plan of a villa at Pompeii.*

The Roman House

◆ Entire houses rarely survive 2,000 years intact. Over the years, houses crumble, are rebuilt, or are torn down to make way for roads, highways, or more modern buildings. In the case of Pompeii, homes were miraculously frozen in the year A.D. 79, buried under tons of mud and ash, just waiting to be discovered by archaeologists. These preserved examples revealed exactly how the citizens of Pompeii lived, right down to the paintings on the walls, the colorful mosaic tile floors, and the pots still on the stove. Historians already knew what the different rooms of a Roman house were because of the many stories and descriptions surviving from Roman times, but the remains of houses at Pompeii brought everything to life and showed how much luxury some families could afford. In the example below, of an actual house in the city, there are over a dozen rooms on the first floor alone, not including hallways.

1. Entrance Hall—This hallway is about 30 feet long. It leads past rooms on either side that might have been shops facing the street.

2. Atrium—This is a partly open courtyard with tiled floors and a drainage pool. The one in the picture is about 30 feet wide and 30 feet long.

The atrium featured columns and decorative objects and was one of the most important rooms in the house. For the rich and powerful, it was a place to receive guests and show off their wealth. Our modern version of an atrium is based on the Roman version—an open space with decorative objects and seating.

3. Small rooms—These had various uses. Stairs led up to more rooms on the second floor.

4. Alae—From the Latin word for "wings," these were also small rooms on either side of the atrium.

5. Hall—This passage led from the atrium further back into the rest of the house, including the cooking and dining areas.

6. Tablinum—This was a room for the family records, similar to a modern office, without the computer.

7. Peristyle—This was another atrium-like room with plants and flowers and an open ceiling in the middle.

8. Triclinum—From the Latin word for "three incliners" or "three couches," this was a dining room with three couches arranged around a table, one perpendicular to the next. The

Romans ate their meals while lying down on their sides on one of the couches in the dining room. They reached out with one hand toward the food on the table and ate lying next to each other, sometimes three or four people to a couch. When a guest was finished eating, he would turn from one side to the other to show he was done.

9. Kitchen—Kitchens had a kind of charcoal stove and additional space to prepare food before cooking.

10. Cubicula—This is Latin for "square"; your parents probably have their own cubicle at work. These are Roman bedrooms, usually pretty small.

First made of stone and later of clay, oil lamps have been used for thousands of years. During Roman times, they were especially popular. They were shaped to give off light by burning liquid animal fat, using a wick of rope or cloth. Some had handles so you could carry them more easily and safely. In this activity, you will make your own oil lamp.

MATERIALS

◇ *1 pound of modeling clay that will harden*
◇ *Scissors*
◇ *Pencil*
◇ *Small metal or plastic spoon*

Break off a piece of clay about the size of your fist. Mold it into a roughly triangular shape about 1½ to 2 inches thick and 3½ inches long, with two equal sides and one side about half as long as the other two. With the scissors, snip off about ¼ inch from the pointy end, at an angle. Using the sharp point of the pencil, bore a hole straight into the center of the clay triangle, beginning at the center of the end you just snipped. Now using the eraser end of the pencil, make a wide hole at the top center of the triangle. You can pick which side you want to be the top. Rotate your wrist to make the hole about ¾ inch wide and almost as deep as the piece of clay. Use your spoon to help you scoop out clay from the hole. Be careful not to hit the bottom and come out the other side! When you are done, you can begin to decorate the lamp. Using the point of your pencil, draw pictures or patterns on the top of the lamp. Some Roman lamps had pictures of people's heads, pictures of animals, or patterned lines and symbols. When you are done, let the clay harden. Now you have a life-sized model of an ancient Roman oil lamp. Don't try to burn anything in it, though. Modern electric light is much safer.

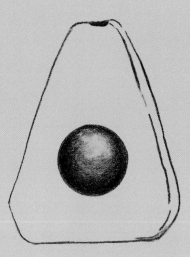

Archaeologists have recovered thousands of these early lamps because they were compact in size and fairly durable. What do you think happens to modern lightbulbs when we throw them out? What are the chances archaeologists in the future will find lightbulbs still in one piece?

Homes of the wealthy also had baths, and sometimes libraries, picture galleries, salons, and rooftop terraces.

Can you measure the size of the rooms in your home's main floor and then draw a floor plan like the one you see for Pompeii? Label each room. Is your home bigger or smaller than the Pompeii house? Which room arrangement do you prefer? The climate of Italy is generally warm and sunny for most of the year, allowing the use of open rooms such as the atrium. Would you be able to have an atrium where you live? How does your bedroom compare in size to the Pompeian bedroom?

Roman Conquests and Defeats

◆ In 146 B.C., the Romans took control of Greece, which had been the most powerful state in the world just three hundred years earlier. The Romans were not too harsh with the Greeks, because after all, much of their inspiration in art, architecture, and science came from the Greeks. Instead, the Romans focused on expanding the empire that the Greeks had begun. They built roads from Rome all across Europe. They sent

▲ *Biblical archaeology tries to verify sites and events mentioned in the Bible. Shown here is the Fountain of Siloam, where Jesus is said to have performed a miracle.*

ships full of soldiers to Britain, Africa, and Asia. Before long, they had built cities and towns in Germany, Hungary, Romania, France, Spain, Israel, Syria, Turkey, England, Scotland, Wales, and Ireland. Many of the artifacts archaeologists find at these sites are spear points, arrowheads, and other military objects made of metal. The

Romans built garrison towns that served as outposts at the edge of enemy territory. The rich and powerful Romans who ruled these foreign provinces built large, luxurious villas that were like palaces, with many rooms and colorful tiled mosaics of Roman life. One such villa was recently discovered in Turkey, and archaeologists had to scramble to try to save as much as they could before the site was flooded by the rising waters of the Euphrates River.

Roman ruins found in the center of the city of Frankfurt, Germany. ▼

Another reason the Roman Empire is of such great interest to archaeologists is because the Romans controlled the land that is now Israel, where many events in both the Old and New Testaments of the Bible took place. Biblical archaeologists study the sites and events mentioned in the Bible, and try to find hard evidence that they really existed or took place. The Roman presence in the Holy Land influenced the way the native people dressed and spent their everyday lives. Under Roman rule, life was not easy for the Jews, who led several uprisings when their traditions were threatened. According to the Bible, after Jesus was born, the Emperor Herod ordered the death of all male children under the age of two. Jesus' parents took him to safety in Egypt until after the death of Herod in 4 B.C.

In the end, the Roman Empire pushed itself to the limit. There were too many territories, too many rich and powerful people, and too much corruption. Slowly, the great empire began to decline. It was difficult to rule so many people and keep them all happy and fed. Many counterfeit coins were circulated, and in some places, about half of the coins archaeologists find are cheap and obvious imitations made by people who hoped the counterfeit money would be accepted as real. In A.D. 286, the emperor Diocletian decided to split the empire into two parts, East and West. The West would be ruled from Rome and the East from Constantinople. Emperors came and went in rapid succession. By the 4th and 5th centuries A.D., bands of barbarians invaded from the east again and again.

Aquincum, a Roman military town in Hungary, was invaded many times during the 4th century, but was rebuilt again and again until the 5th century, when the fierce Huns and other invaders drove away the last of the Romans. This happened all over the empire; after a while, waves of barbarians from northern and eastern Europe and Asia, along with disease and poverty, put an end to the Western Roman Empire. In fact, some people actually preferred living under the barbarians to the ways of the Romans.

How do you think archaeologists could determine the end of the Roman Empire by looking at artifacts? For one thing, they would not find any more coins—the great mints in Rome and all over Europe shut down not long after A.D. 400. Villas and whole towns were sometimes abandoned, or looted and destroyed by barbarians. Dating of artifacts at Roman sites proves that Roman influence died off during the 5th century A.D. Different types of artifacts appearing during the 4th and 5th centuries at a Roman site prove that invaders had taken over and settled there— for example, the famous fine and colorful Roman

▲ *Roman glass production ended in the West with the fall of the empire during the 4th century A.D.*

glass production ended with the fall of the empire. Though the Eastern Roman Empire flourished and became known as the Byzantine Empire, the great classical Roman civilization of the West was finished for good.

Just as the great and powerful civilizations in Europe, Asia, and Africa were dying off, some of the most spectacular and mighty civilizations were being built in the Americas, as you'll see in the next chapter.

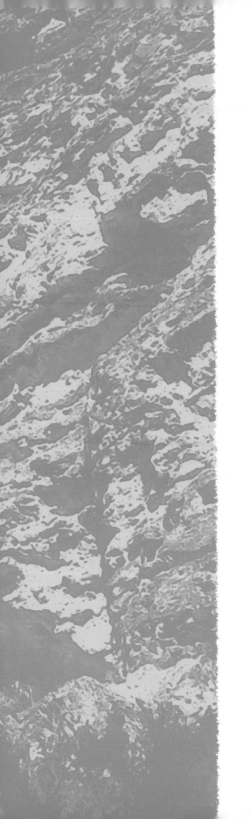

6 The New World

A group of people stood facing the broad horizon. It was a cold day, like most others during the Ice Age in the Northern Hemisphere, but the air was dry. Snow had not fallen for weeks. The ice was not very bad in the area, and even though there were a few glaciers, they were small and several miles in the distance. The group knew they needed to move on. There hadn't been many animals to hunt lately, since they had probably moved on to better land. As the group moved forward, they could not possibly realize they would be the first humans to ever set foot in what is now the Americas.

Australopithecus, *Homo habilis*, *Homo erectus*, and the Neanderthals had all come and gone without ever having lived anywhere in the Americas. Modern *Homo sapiens* spent the first 30,000 years of his existence in Africa, Asia, and Europe, before venturing to North America. The lower sea level during the Ice Age made it easy for the group 15,000 years ago. What is now known as the Bering Strait, the water between the northeastern tip of Asia and the western tip of Alaska, was dry land at that time. Once the group crossed over, others followed. What they found was an ice-free corridor leading through Alaska and south, all the way to what is now Colorado and Arizona. From there it was easy enough to get to Central and South America. The group and those who followed them were the ancestors of all the major tribes and civilizations in the Americas. Once the Ice Age ended and the sea level rose again, the Bering land bridge was submerged under more than 100 feet of water. Within a few thousand years the human population had multiplied and were living in almost every habitable corner of North and South America.

Life went on in the rest of the world, and civilizations were born and died in Europe, Asia, and Africa. None of these people had any idea a "New World" existed until 1,000 years ago, when the Vikings arrived. For many years people thought Christopher Columbus was the first to reach the Americas, but more than 400 years before Columbus was even born, the Vikings had set sail across the northern Atlantic from Scandinavia and landed at what is now Newfoundland, Canada. Archaeologists found the proof at a site called L'Anse Aux Meadows.

One reason the Vikings' presence in the New World went unproven for so long was because the Vikings did not stay. Disease, the severe climate, and attacks by natives sent them home after only a few years. Though their American settlement was a failure, the Vikings flourished in northern Europe, settled Iceland, and frequently attacked many parts of Europe about 1,000 years ago, including Normandy, in France, and England.

As European countries became more powerful and ambitious, they opened up new trade routes to the East, where exotic spices and riches awaited. Little by little, explorers ventured out into the vast world. First, they stayed close to the coastlines of Europe and Africa. Columbus first crossed the Atlantic Ocean in 1492 and made several trips back and forth. Amerigo Vespucci sailed across the Atlantic in 1499 and returned in 1501. Vespucci mapped and explored thousands of miles of coastline and devised a system to figure out the circumference of the earth. Unlike Columbus, he believed the land he was exploring was truly a new world, not the easternmost part of Asia. By 1507, a mapmaker referred to the new continent as America in honor of Vespucci.

Once the European powers accepted that there really was a new world, they had two new goals—to find a navigable shortcut through the continent to get to Asia, and to conquer and exploit the people they came across in the process. Though Columbus's trips did not yield very much gold or treasure, the adventurers were hopeful there was treasure to be had somewhere in the Americas.

The Aztecs and Inca

◆ By 1519, the Spaniard Hernán Cortés had arrived in Mexico with about 500 soldiers and was met by members of the Aztec civilization. The Aztecs were an advanced civilization that controlled a great area of land in what is now Mexico. Their capital city, Tenochtitlán, was built on an island in the middle of Lake Texcoco, using landfill to expand the island, and with a series of canals and causeways running through it. The roughly 200,000 people who lived in Tenochtitlán were fed by the many rectangular floating gardens called *chinampas*. Other cultures feared the Aztecs and offered them massive amounts of tribute—gifts of food, cotton cloaks, highly prized exotic bird feathers, and gold. The Aztecs were

also believers in human sacrifice to the gods. On occasion, thousands of people were killed at a time.

Aztec legend described a mythical figure named Quetzalcóatl, who had left Mexico hundreds of years before and promised to return in the very same year that Cortés arrived. The Aztecs believed this exotic-looking man, riding a strange four-legged beast they had never seen before, to be none other than their returned hero. Who else could he possibly be? They showered him and his men with gold, at which the Spaniards looked with wide eyes. Cortés marched inland to the capital city of Tenochtitlán, located at the site of present-day Mexico City. Cortés captured and tortured the Aztec leader Montezuma until he was nearly dead, as a way to frighten and collapse the Aztec civilization. The Spaniards then tortured and killed Montezuma's successor, Guatemozin. The Aztecs succeeded in killing some of the Spaniards, but reinforcements arrived from Cuba, and the Spanish soldiers were able to defeat the Aztecs, who fought bitterly to the very end.

Francisco Pizarro arrived in Peru with the same idea as Cortés, to trick and destroy the civilization and take whatever he could. In the city of Caxamalco, Pizarro tricked the Incan leader Atahuallpa into trusting him, took him captive, held him for ransom, and killed him. This must have been a terrible shock to the eight million

Incas in the empire who saw him as a living god. Within only a few years of the arrival of the Spaniards, the Aztec civilization in Mexico and the Inca civilization in Peru were both destroyed by murder and disease.

Unfortunately, most of the gold artworks that were stolen are gone, long since melted into ingots or bars that were shipped back to Europe and used for other purposes. Spain was not interested in opening a museum of American civilization. Whatever beauty they saw in the gold and jewels, they thought the treasure would be more easily shipped and counted as bars. Added together, more than five billion dollars worth of treasure was taken away from the Inca and Aztecs. Luckily, before they destroyed the Inca and the Aztecs completely, the Spanish conquerors were able to record information about some of the cities, people, sculptures, artwork, and stories they came across. After the conquest, the Spaniards continued to seek a steady source of gold and silver, forcing men and women alike to work long hours in the dangerous mines. The population thinned out due to the death and illness of the miners, who sometimes were made to work naked in cold water.

In their occupation of Peru and Mexico, the Spaniards were not very interested in any ruins or remains they came across, so little new was discovered about the Incas and Aztecs until recently. Archaeologists in the late 19th and early 20th centuries began scientific excavations in Peru and elsewhere to find the remains of the once great civilizations. In 1911, the archaeologist Hiram Bingham found the lost town of Machu Picchu, high up in the Andes Mountains. The Inca were expert builders who used precisely carved stones that fit together like pieces of a puzzle, without any mortar. They also created a network of thousands of miles of high-quality paved roads to connect all the cities and villages of their large empire. Since many of their cities were in the mountains, they used a special form of agriculture that was suited to mountain life. They leveled off a series of steps into the mountainsides and planted their crops on these terraces.

A wooden drinking cup from Peru dating to the 1500s. ▶

▲ *The "lost" Incan city of Machu Picchu.*

▲ *Agriculture on a Peruvian mountainside using terracing.*

Excavations in Peru have also revealed many other cultures besides the Inca. Pottery, textiles, and statues have all been uncovered in the last 100 years. Excavations in the mountains 200 miles northeast of Lima, Peru, have uncovered the remains of the Chavin civilization, with a large temple complex, intricately carved statues of animals and gods, and colorful textiles. Because some parts of Peru are still fairly remote and unpopulated, new discoveries continue to be made into the 21st century.

◇◇◇◇◇◇◇◇◇◇◇◇◇◇◇◇◇◇◇◇◇◇

The Maya

◆ In Central America, there was another civilization that was conquered by Spain. These people didn't receive the same attention because they did not offer as many riches and their civilization was already falling apart by the time the Spaniards arrived. Classical Mayan civilization peaked between A.D. 250 and A.D. 900, and then declined as its population grew and food became more scarce. Some large Mayan cities collapsed, and Mayan civilization continued on a smaller scale in places like the Yucatán Peninsula on the eastern coast of Mexico, until the arrival of the Spanish in the 1540s. The Maya fought back, but were finally defeated in 1546.

Just as with the Aztecs and Inca, the Mayan civilization was mostly forgotten until a lawyer turned archaeologist named John Lloyd Stephens read a report mentioning strange ruins in Central America. Using his connections, Stephens got an official appointment as a United States diplomatic representative to Central America. He

Primary Context

In the barren desert areas on the coast of Peru, surface survey is the best and easiest way for archaeologists to figure out where to excavate. Few people have ventured near these inhospitable places since the time when they were abandoned, so pottery and stone fragments lie where they were left. Without decaying plants or rain, floods, and erosion to move and cover the sites, artifacts are more likely to stay on the surface of the ground. Archaeologists call this primary context, *because the artifacts are in the original place where they were left. When someone or something has moved artifacts from their primary context to somewhere else, it is called* secondary context. *An example of this would be if grave robbers disturbed a grave site and moved artifacts.*

could now go in search of the ruins and use the government to fund his trip. Before he left the United States, he recruited his friend, an artist named Frederick Catherwood, to accompany him on the journey.

When they arrived in 1839, they cut their way through the thick jungle until they came across marvelous ruins of stone temples 100 feet in height, carved statues, and ball courts—all long since abandoned. Catherwood sketched hundreds of highly detailed drawings of what he saw, though complaining about the poor lighting and the hard-to-copy pictures and figures on the stones. Stephens and Catherwood published the story of their adventures, causing quite a sensation in America and Europe. Who were the mysterious people that built such great temples and had a strange system of writing in pictures or glyphs? Stephens thought they had to be highly civilized in order to build such large-scale monuments, but some people were still not happy to accept the idea that civilizations could have existed in America before the Europeans arrived.

Though Stephens and Catherwood were not able to reach every site, nor decipher the Mayan writing, they opened the way for archaeologists to come in and excavate. Today, sites at Tikal, Palenque, Lamanai, Chichén Itzá, Tulum, Copán, and many others have all been excavated and cleared of vines and trees so tourists can visit. Only 30 years ago, excavations at Cuello, Belize,

▲ *The Mayan Jaguar Temple at Lamanai, Belize.*

proved that Mayan civilization had its beginnings as far back as 2500 B.C. There are so many Mayan sites that excavations are still ongoing.

Catherwood and Stephens noticed many large statues and temples during their voyages through Mayan country. They also noticed some smaller, portable statuettes and other items. Archaeologists call the small, portable items made or modified by humans or humanlike creatures *artifacts,*

While pottery is one of the most common artifacts at almost any site, prehistoric or historic, you can imagine how rare it is to find a whole vessel that has survived the centuries unbroken. This is especially true for glass jars and bottles, which have been made for more than 2,000 years but almost never survive intact. Archaeologists mostly find fragments, ranging in size from most of a pot to tiny shards less than an inch long. You can figure out the circumference of a bottle or jar, and therefore what it might have held, even if you have only a small fragment.

MATERIALS
- *Pencil*
- *Tracing paper*
- *Compass*
- *Ruler*

With your pencil, trace the outlines of the two fragments, A and B, onto the tracing paper. Now fasten the pencil to the compass. Experiment with different arcs until you find the one that exactly matches the curve of Fragment A, then draw the rest of the circle. Using the ruler measure the *diameter*, the distance from one side to the other, through the middle of the circle where the sharp point of the compass was. Now do the same for Fragment B. Judging by their sizes, which of the following items do you think Fragment A might have held and which might Fragment B have held—perfume, wine, olives, grapes, wheat flour, coins, or stone blocks?

A

B

while larger, nonportable human-made items are called *features*. Any animal or plant remains that were used by people, either for eating or decoration, are called *ecofacts*. Go outside and look around. Can you find at least four features, four artifacts, and four ecofacts that a future archaeologist might find where you live?

▲ *Mayan artwork, drawn by Frederick Catherwood.*

◀ *A ceremonial scene from the wall of the Mayan palace at Palenque, drawn by Catherwood.*

The climate in the deserts of Peru is particularly good for preserving artifacts, since the dry weather helps keep organic materials from decaying. Organic material is anything that was once alive, including plant remains and animal remains and anything made from plant or animal remains—

▲ *This piece of ancient textile from Peru is more than 2,000 years old. Organic materials such as cloth survive best under dry and unchanging conditions.*

like a book, a leather briefcase, or a cotton T-shirt. Several well-preserved human mummies and strips of brightly colored fabric have been found in Peru. The dry climate there desiccates, or dries out, organic remains by taking away all their moisture.

Other good climates for preserving artifacts are those where the temperature does not change too much. Constant temperature helps keep organic matter stable (like the extreme cold of the Swiss Alps, where the frozen ice-man nicknamed Oetzi was found). Temperate climates, where it is hot in the summer and cold in the winter, are the worst for organic artifacts. The heat and cold expand and contract the artifacts, causing them to crack and buckle. In fact, potholes in roads happen for similar reasons.

Moisture is bad because it harbors bacteria and insects that eat away at organic remains until there is nothing left for archaeologists to find. Sometimes, underwater conditions are good for preservation, in places like bogs and swamps, where something called tannic acid stabilizes organic remains.

See if you can figure out which of the following artifacts you would likely excavate in good condition. The first trick is to figure out which artifacts

are organic and which are not. Remember, non-organic artifacts have a much better chance of surviving in any climate.

1. *a New York Times newspaper from the 1800s in New York City*
2. *a clay pipe in Virginia*
3. *a glass bottle in Mexico*
4. *a wooden spear in a glacier*
5. *a leather shoe in the desert of Peru*
6. *a brick in your backyard*
7. *a 500-year-old ear of corn in a tropical jungle*
8. *a plastic spoon in California*
9. *a dead squirrel in a swamp or bog*

Answer: (1) No; (2) Yes; (3) Yes; (4) Yes; (5) Yes; (6) Yes; (7) No; (8) Yes; (9) Yes

North American Natives

◆ Archaeologists have realized the New World held hundreds of different cultures besides the major civilizations everyone has heard about—the Aztec, Maya, and Inca. Throughout North America, natives adapted to their environments, finding the best places and ways to live. In the hot and dry American southwest, mud brick, or *adobe*, pueblos were common while in the northeast, longhouses made of sticks and tree bark were preferred. In the mountains of the west, the native Americans built their homes into cliffs where they could be sheltered from the cold and the wind.

Most natives in North America went through a sad period in their history as they were exploited and pushed out of their homelands, just like their distant relatives in Central and South America. The natives were no match for the technology and the disease-carrying people of a rapidly growing United States. By the early 1900s, the remaining native populations in the country were sent to live in specially set-aside land called *reservations*. The Smithsonian Institution, founded in 1846, was able to collect and preserve everyday Native American items such as pottery and clothing. Many of these items are now part of the collection of the National Museum of the American Indian. When you look at Native American artifacts, you have to see if they were precontact or postcontact with Europeans. You may have seen pictures of Native Americans holding guns, sitting high up on the backs of mighty horses. Though this was accurate during the 1800s, the natives had no guns or horses until the Europeans introduced them in the 1500s.

Even though much has changed since the days before the Europeans arrived, excavations show some traditions have remained the same for many hundreds of years. Cultural anthropologists can study and interview Native Americans who live on reservations and find out about their customs, stories, and traditions. Archaeologists can then compare what the cultural anthropologists have discovered to what their excavations reveal. Surprisingly, through all the hardships of the last 400 years, Native American culture—their customs, beliefs, and traditions—survives to this day.

Native Americans lived in North America for more than 10,000 years before the Europeans arrived, so it is not shocking their artifacts turn up in almost every place imaginable. The pioneering farmers who moved from Pennsylvania and New York to Ohio, Iowa, Missouri, and Illinois turned up all kinds of Indian artifacts—arrowheads, hand axes, and other tools—as they plowed their fields. Thomas Jefferson, the future president, was fascinated by a seven-foot-high mound he found in Virginia. Always an innova-

You've learned that each layer of soil is generally older than the one on top of it. It is not always so simple in the real world. Natural stratigraphy can be interrupted by animals burrowing into the ground, by tree roots, or by earthquakes; and by people digging canals, tunnels, foundations, graves, or wells, or making trash mounds and garbage dumps.

MATERIALS
◆ Pencil
◆ Pad of paper

Using the picture on the right, try to put the artifacts labeled A–F in order of their age, from oldest to newest.

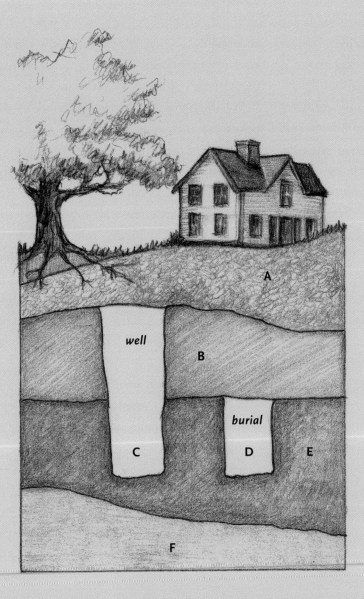

ANSWERS: F (oldest), E, D, B, C, A (newest)

tor, Jefferson himself excavated a trench into the center of the burial mound. He found bones and stone artifacts in several layers and was able to understand there was a stratigraphy, or layering of the earth, in place that showed the artifacts had been deposited in several stages. Though Heinrich Schliemann was the first professional archaeologist to use the principles of stratigraphy in a large-scale excavation, Jefferson was the first person to recognize the importance of the dif-

▲ *The houses of the cliff dwellers are some of the most fascinating archaeological remains in the Americas. Shown is Montezuma's Palace, a 20-room cliff dwelling of the Sinagua culture in Arizona, dating from the 1100s.*

ferent layers. He was also the first person to show a real interest in the artifacts of the North American Indians.

Hundreds of digs are now conducted every year at prehistoric sites all across the United States. The artifacts recovered help us understand how Native Americans lived—what they ate, what they wore, who their friends and enemies were, and when they died out or moved to other sites. As archaeologists and cultural anthropologists have discovered, there were many different tribes and groups of Native Americans, each with its own customs and unique way of living.

▲ *The long-abandoned remains of adobe buildings from the Hohokam culture have been found in the city of Phoenix, Arizona.*

Even though parts of their rich history have been destroyed, the customs and traditions of the original inhabitants of the Americas will never completely fade away, because of the many lasting impressions they have made on us and because of their strong presence in the Americas today. How many state names can you count that you think are Indian names? Minnesota and Missouri are two examples. Look on a map and find rivers, lakes, and cities you think might be Indian words. Do you eat corn, potatoes, sweet potatoes, peanuts, chocolate, maple syrup, pumpkin, or squash? All of these crops were first harvested by native peoples of the Americas.

From the time Europeans landed and traded with the Indians, the archaeology of the Americas is no longer considered prehistoric archaeology. After they arrived, the Europeans documented the stories of their lives, their surroundings, and the people they came across in writing. As you will see in the next chapter, the archaeology of well-documented times is called historical archaeology.

◇◇◇◇◇◇◇◇◇◇◇◇◇◇◇◇◇◇◇◇◇◇◇

7 Historical Archaeology

It is lunchtime on a Thursday in downtown New York City, and men and women in business suits scurry along streets between the thousand-foot-high, steel-and-glass skyscrapers in which they work, dodging veering taxicabs and impatient drivers left and right. The sun beats down on the concrete sidewalks and asphalt pavement, making it feel even hotter than it is. Soon lunch hour will be over, though, and it will be time for them to step back into elevators that will whisk them up 60 or 70 floors to their air-conditioned offices.

▲ *Beaver Street, New York City, today.*

If you could step into a time machine and come out 350 years ago at that very same spot, you might think you were on some other planet. Where the cars and people and office towers stood would be nothing more than a few one-story, red brick homes with yellow brick trim and red tiled roofs, and maybe some pigs and sheep roaming the dirt streets. A wealthy Dutch burgher might be seen strolling by, puffing on a long-stemmed white clay pipe, his silver shoe buckles glistening in the sun. A Native American might even be seen walking into town with some furs, trying to trade for Dutch beads or tools.

What a dramatic change!

Still, if you decided to return to the present at the normal speed of time, you would wind up in

▲ *Beaver Street, New York City, 1679.*

▲ *Bits of clay pipes are among the most common artifacts at 17th- and 18th-century Dutch sites in the Americas. This illustration shows Dutch men smoking the very long-stemmed pipes.*

the 21st century seeing how gradually change happens, and in some cases, not even noticing when things change. Historical archaeologists are trained to notice the slightest change in an artifact. A decrease of 1/64 inch in the width of a clay pipe's stem can mean that it is 50 years newer than a thicker pipe stem. A slight difference in the way the lip of a glass bottle is shaped can mean 100 years. As you can imagine, it is not easy work, especially when there may be hundreds of thousands of pipe fragments or bottle lips to measure and record.

◇◇◇◇◇◇◇◇◇◇◇◇◇◇◇◇◇◇◇◇◇◇◇◇◇◇

Old Buildings

The historical value of a building is not always easy to determine. Sometimes, in a neighborhood where most of the buildings are 100 years old, a 75-year-old building is not so important, but in a neighborhood where most of the buildings are only 25 years old, a 75-year-old building might be very important.

Do you know any old buildings in your neighborhood? How old is the apartment building or house you live in? Have any old buildings near you been demolished recently? If you don't know the answers to these questions, try asking your parents or going to the local library. Libraries often have newspaper clippings and maps that show the history of a town.

Once you find some of the oldest buildings in your neighborhood, try to make a list of how those buildings are different from the newer ones. What are they made of? What do they look like? Make a chart to show the results of your research.

So why do we care about historical archaeology anyway?

We care because the most fascinating mysteries are not always the oldest mysteries. Did you ever wonder what life was like for your grandparents or great-grandparents when they were growing up? What kind of toys did they play with? What kind of houses did they live in and what kind of clothes did they wear?

Sometimes, the recent past is more fascinating to us than the distant past because we have more of a connection with the recent past. Historical archaeology helps us understand what life was like as early as the year 1500, and as recently as 50 years ago.

Unlike prehistorical archaeologists, historical archaeologists have extra help when they do their research. Because they are dealing with the recent past, historical archaeologists have maps, old documents, and books available to give them clues as to what they might find and where they might find it. In other words, they have *written history* of the time period they are researching. This is why the archaeology of the last few hundred years is called historical archaeology, because there exist written accounts and paintings and descriptions of life, and some of the tools, toys, houses, and clothing of the people who lived in those times.

Historical archaeologists often have more specific questions than do prehistorical archaeologists. For example, we know a lot about the life of President Thomas Jefferson, but until recently we knew nothing about the living conditions of his slaves. Archaeologists excavated old slave quarters at the presidential home of Monticello and found many remnants of slave life in early 19th-century Virginia. Because Jefferson was president, archaeologists were more curious about his slaves than they would have been about an ordinary man's slaves.

Historical archaeology can answer many questions about recent history. Where exactly was a particular Revolutionary War battle fought? What kind of toys did the children of Jamestown, Virginia, play with? Did the pioneers of the Old West smoke and drink a lot? How much trade occurred between European settlers and Native Americans in the early days of the Pilgrims? How were the ships of the great explorers built more than 400 years ago? What did the inside of the *Titanic* really look like?

The list of questions is only limited by our curiosity. Many have already been answered, and many more still wait to be answered by future archaeologists—maybe even you!

The funny thing is, people were not always interested in their recent past. Historic buildings were often demolished and not many people cared. As time passed, people slowly became more aware of the beauty and insight things from the past could offer. In the 1960s, when the old Pennsylvania Train Station in New York City was demolished, so many people were outraged it led to the creation of the Landmarks Preservation Commission. Still, many beautiful old buildings slip through these protections and are demolished anyway.

Looking to the Past

◆ Historical archaeologists are often called in to help reconstruct the past when people are trying to restore old buildings that have been neglected, or to dig at the site of a long-gone, famous old building.

The usefulness of historical archaeologists depends on the area. If you want to study North Dakota in the 1600s, you will not need a historical archaeologist because there were no Europeans there at the time, and therefore no recorded history of the area. Though Native Americans often passed down an oral history of life and the history of their peoples, historical archaeologists would have no hard facts or dates to work with. On the other hand, if you wanted to study historical archaeology of Massachusetts in the 1600s, you could do so because the Pilgrims landed there in 1620 and recorded the story of their lives in journals and other documents.

If you asked a historical archaeologist what was the single most important invention of the last 1,000 years, the answer would probably be the printing press. A good historical archaeologist might spend many hours in the library looking at old books and maps.

In the distant past, each book had to be handwritten and any illustrations had to be done from scratch for each copy of the book that was made. Each letter of a word was drawn one at a time. Colorful inks were painstakingly used to decorate the margins of these books. Only the richest and most powerful people could afford these "illuminated" books.

When Johannes Gutenberg rolled the first book through his mechanical printing press in the year 1454, it was the beginning of a new era. Type was set into blocks and inked, then pressed to paper. Even though books were still very expensive for more than a hundred years after that, and most common people did not know how to read anyway, the printing press allowed the mass production of all kinds of books. Old stories, legends, and histories were retold again, many available for the first time to the public. New histories, biographies, and journals were written. The printing of weekly and daily newspapers was made possible.

Drawings could also be reproduced through the printing press, and so early firsthand pictures of lost civilizations such as the Aztec, the Inca, and the Maya still exist. Cheap copies of maps could be made, to allow travelers and explorers an easy way to find their destination. Some of these maps from the 16th, 17th, 18th, and 19th centuries help modern archaeologists find long-lost historic sites around the world.

Another important invention that helped historical archaeologists was the photocopy machine. Now, when visiting local libraries, they could take home an exact duplicate of the historic maps or documents they were studying, without spending hours taking notes or tracing lines. Today, the Internet allows even quicker access to documents, which are scanned and placed on Web sites such as the U.S. Library of Congress' "American Memory" site. Try it yourself—type in **http://memory.loc.gov**. This site has maps, photos, and even early short films from the 1890s. There are also collections of some of the great presidents—documents relating to Washington, Jefferson, and Lincoln are all online, part of more than 250,000 scanned images you can see. Go to the "Collection Finder, Maps" section and perform a keyword search to find a November 1862 aerial view of Fredricksburg, Virginia. Zoom in to the lower right of the map. What are the people doing?

The Library of Congress is a good starting point, but other Web sites also have similar types of documents available online. With a few clicks of a mouse you can find laws, deeds, and maps in full detail. Technology is definitely a friend to the historical archaeologist.

Historical archaeology is important for all archaeologists to understand, even if they are mainly interested in what happened 5,000 years ago, because chances are good that before getting to the ground level or "living floor" of 5,000 years ago, they will come across remnants of more recent life. Throughout human history, people

A view of Paris as it appeared in 1730. Historic archaeologists use maps and views to help them pinpoint where buildings stood. ▼

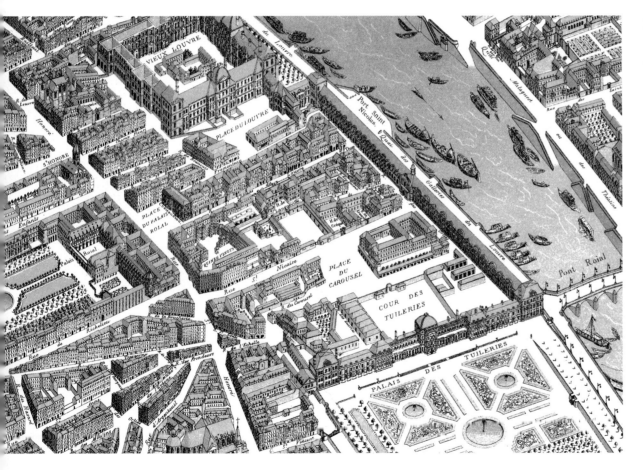

For as long as humans have been drawing, they have been making maps of the places they live. Mapmaking, or cartography, really took off during the time of great exploration, beginning in the mid- to late 15th century. Archaeologists can pinpoint the location of a site by comparing present-day maps with centuries-old maps.

In this activity, look below at the old map of the City of Philadelphia in 1862 and the map of present-day Philadelphia. Find the Independence Mall, where Independence Hall and the Liberty Bell are located, on today's map. Now try to find it on the 1862 map. If you have trouble, use other landmarks common to both maps to help you. It did

not exist yet, did it? Now find Delaware Avenue, along the Delaware River, on the old map. Can you find it on the new map? What has happened to the waterfront in the years since 1862? What would you be able to say about the date of an archaeological site found on Penn's Landing—would it be from before 1862 or after 1862?

Philadelphia in 1862.

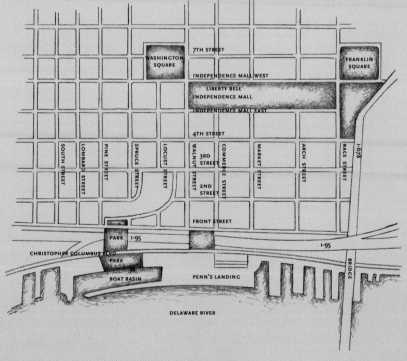

Philadelphia today.

have tended to choose the same places to live that their ancestors did. A good place to live in 1900 was probably also a good place to live in 1900 B.C., especially if natural features like rivers, streams, and hills have not changed in that time.

Explorers and Colonists

◆ The most important events of the historic era, besides the invention of the printing press, involve the exploration of the New World and other distant places unseen by Europeans. Beginning in the late 15th century, the competition began to really heat up to find the shortest route to India and the Spice Islands of the Pacific. Columbus, da Gama, Magellan, Cortés, Vespucci, Verrazano, and Hudson all sailed the dangerous, unknown seas in different directions with the same hopes: to find fame and vast riches.

Some, like Magellan, were killed en route. Others, like Hudson, disappeared at sea. As you read in the last chapter, still others found gold and fortune at the expense of native peoples of Central and South America. What many explorers eventually came to accept was that there was no real shortcut to India and China, and that while the New World had some treasures, its main value was in the endless land it offered.

Before long, missionaries, political and religious refugees, like the Pilgrims, and people simply in search of a huge profit had all made the long and dangerous journey across the Atlantic to the New World. They settled in Mexico, California, and Florida during the 1500s, and Virginia, Delaware, Maryland, New Jersey, New York, Massachusetts, Montreal, and Quebec during the early 1600s.

British, French, Dutch, and Spanish colonies sprang up all over the place and struggled to make it through each year. In the South, colonists had to put up with heat, humidity, and diseases like malaria. In the North, colonists were lucky to make it through the severe New England winters. Some colonies failed completely. In 1583, a colony on the coast of chilly Newfoundland, Canada, failed. There is also the famous story of the Roanoke settlement in North Carolina. In 1587, Sir Walter Raleigh found more than 100 people willing to settle on the coast of what is now North Carolina. When a supply ship sailed into port a few years later, the crew found that the entire colony had vanished without a trace.

By 1750, colonies were well established throughout North, South, and Central America, the Caribbean, as well as many parts of Asia and Africa. The period from 1650 to 1750, when the colonies were first appearing and becoming large and powerful, are of great interest to archaeologists. Digs have been conducted all over the

What sites are the easiest to find? Pretend you are an archaeologist. Which of the following sites would you be more likely to find without much trouble?

SITE 1

A campsite in the woods used by three people one summer night in 1910.

SITE 2

The site where 40,000 troops crossed the Weser River in August 1761.

Though you might automatically think the number of people passing through the site is an important factor, it might not be so important. First, if there is currently a city built over Site 2 and Site 1 is still untouched forest, it will be easier to find Site 1. Now think about what happened at Site 1 and Site 2. At Site 1, as you can see, the campers built a fire, fished, and probably cooked and ate food. There may be remains of the hearth, animal bones, and other garbage. On the other hand, the 40,000 troops probably crossed the river in a few minutes. At most, maybe one or two soldiers lost a button or a fragment of a boot heel.

For Site 1, you have an old photograph to help you find the spot of the campsite. For Site 2, all you have is a general idea, within a few miles, of where the river was crossed.

▲ *Camping in the forest, 1910.*

moved herch when fhe fees them repent, in hopes that fhe may not be obliged to abide by her word.

Thurfday, Auguft 20.

Holzminden, Auguft 6.

THE French in this neighbourhood and that of Hoxter, have been confiderably reinforced; they are fuppofed to be already 40,000 ftrong. They are commanded by the Duke de Broglio. The probability increafes every day, that they will crofs the Wefer in this country. Another corps of 12,000 French have taken poft at Blomberg.

Minden, Aug. 6. Prince Ferdinand feems, for important fecret reafons, not to oppofe M. Broglio's army, which is again advancing, after making an evolution.

Head-quarters of the Hereditary Prince at Dorf-Bremen, Aug. 4. Yefterday the Prince had a conference of half an hour, between our advanced pofts and thofe of the Marfhal de Soubize, on indifferent fubjects, with the Prince of Condé, who defired this interview to be acquainted with the Hereditary Prince.

SCOTLAND.

Edinburgh, Aug. 15. Wednefday forenoon was married here ——

▲ *Newspaper account of 1761 tells of troop movements.*

world, revealing thousands and thousands of artifacts—everything from clay pipes, beautiful ceramics, colored bottles, silver and gold coins, jewelry, belt and shoe buckles, to whole houses and ships.

These historic treasures tell us a lot about the early days in colonies. Because colonies were often so far from the country from which the settlers originally came, and hardly had any industry for the first 50 or so years, archaeologists are always interested in tracing where the artifacts they find at these sites were made. This knowledge would show the popular trade routes of the time and can reveal all kinds of relationships between different countries. As time passed and colonies became more independent, more of the things they needed in their everyday lives were made right where they lived; yet some of the finer, more expensive items such as wine, ceramics, or jewelry continued to be imported from "home" or other countries.

By the 1800s, technology was changing. Many common items were now machine-made. Remember the bottle lips mentioned at the beginning of the chapter? Archaeologists can tell if bottles were mouth blown free-form, mouth blown into a mold, or machine-made in a mold, based on the appearance of the bottle. The same applies to many everyday things: the smoother, rounder, and more uniformly made, the better the technology and the newer the item.

As technology grew, people were able to travel farther in less time. Beginning in the 1840s, the railroad opened up vast unsettled parts of North America. Towns sprang up along the routes of these early trains. If the rail line went bankrupt or if the station closed, people abandoned the area, creating "ghost towns." These ghost towns are good places to dig because they haven't been disturbed for a long time. Other ghost towns were created after the gold and silver rushes, starting in 1848 in California, Montana, Idaho, Nevada, and Canada. Once the gold or silver ore ran out,

Bottle lips from the 1800s found in Warwick, New York ▼

the many towns were abandoned within a few months.

The Civil War

◆ The Civil War is another popular 19th-century subject for archaeologists. There were thousands of sites created during the war—battlefields, stockades, prisons, and encampments—and most are still unexcavated. Everything from buttons, bullets, and belt buckles to whole cannons have been uncovered. At the Andersonville Prison Camp, a failed escape tunnel was found! To help preserve these places and keep them from being developed, the U.S. government has named many of these places National Historic Battlefields.

All through the 19th century, the historic record got better and better. More precise maps were drawn and more books were written, everything from detailed histories to colorful biographies. There are many thousands of books, diaries, photos, and drawings of the Civil War, but archaeology can still add to our knowledge. A good historical archaeologist knows to keep an open mind—you never know when what you find is going to contradict what the records say. There is an old saying that goes, "History is written by the winners." You can probably guess what this means—that if you read a book about the Revolutionary War you are reading our side—the winning side—of the story. If England had won the war, then they would be running the country and writing the books we read in school. A good archaeologist can compare what the excavation reveals about an event against what books and maps say, and see what the differences are.

And even all the books in the world can't tell you as much about what Civil War bullets looked like as finding a bullet at a dig can tell you. A picture really can be worth a thousand words. When an archaeologist combines what the books say with an actual artifact, much more can be learned than with either thing by itself. When a soldier writes in his diary about how he saw the shell fragments, or *shrapnel*, from a cannonball kill one of his friends, you can believe it. But when you find a piece of the shrapnel, you can imagine it.

Historical archaeology is about getting such a complete picture of what life was like, you feel that you could close your eyes and be there, 150 years ago. Many museums around the world use historical archaeology to create lifelike displays and recreations of 17th-, 18th-, and 19th-century life.

How can tree rings be used by archaeologists to date houses, or even entire villages?

First, scientists "core" the oldest living trees in many areas, taking only very thin slivers to show all the rings of each tree trunk without really damaging the trees. Going backward from the present, the outermost ring, a year is assigned to each ring on each core. The thickness of a ring depends on how much rain fell that year and how hot or cold the temperatures were. What do you think a ring will look like in a hot, dry year? All trees in an area will show the same patterns, because they have all experienced the same weather conditions. Before the 1900s, most houses were built using wood from local trees, so this dating method works on most older buildings. The method has been used successfully on pieces of wood as ancient as 1,300 years old. Now it is your turn to try this method out.

Imagine you are a historical archaeologist working on an old property in rural western Massachusetts. You are digging at the site of the Smyth House, rumored to have been built in 1650. Not much is left of the grand old house, except for a rotting floor, two walls, and a few thick, old oak beams. Behind the remains of the house is a small barn, also made from rough-cut boughs of wood that look quite old. You are excited, because you can take a core sample of the beams and try to compare it to the master *dendrochronologic* (tree ring chronology) record; but when you call around, you find that for some reason, there are no tree ring records of this area.

You are very disappointed, until you notice, lying on the property, the trunk of what was once a gigantic maple tree. During a trip to the local historical society, you get lucky and find an old photo of two women standing next to the fallen tree trunk. On the back of the picture it says "The 10th anniversary of the Big Storm, Sunday, September 22, 19—9." The problem is you can't make out that very faded second-to-last digit of the date. Looking carefully at the photo, is there any way you can tell what year the picture was taken? Can you get any clues from the way the person is dressed? Look at the hats—have you ever heard the term "flappers" before? How about looking at a perpetual calendar? There are 14 different calendars that we use on a rotating basis. For example, the exact calendar used in the year 2000 will not be used again until 2028. If you have an almanac nearby, you can check to see in which years ending in "9" the date September 22 fell on a Sunday.

Now that you know the year is 1929, the next thing you do is get a core sample from the old tree trunk and date the rings back in time from 1919 (the year we assume that the big storm ripped out the tree). You take the core samples from the house and barn and try to match them up with the newly made "master core" from the giant tree stump.

To do this, make a photocopy of this page and cut out the three strips. Try to align the house and barn strips with the master core strip. What years were the house and the barn built? In what types of places around the world would this method of dating be impossible to use?

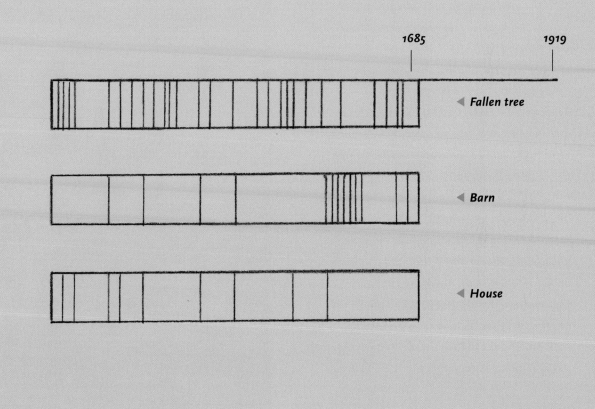

1685   1919

◀ Fallen tree

◀ Barn

◀ House

The African Burial Ground

In 1991, Edward Rutsch and other archaeologists in New York City turned up what was the forgotten African Burial Ground, a 7-acre 18th-century graveyard for 20,000 of the city's African Americans. The cemetery was used for 80 years, beginning in about 1712, until the land was sold and developed. The burials survived for 200 years because they were covered with about 25 feet of landfill and rubble. Over the last 200 years, whenever a new building was built, the foundations never got low enough to hit the burial layer. Only when a new federal building was going to be built were archaeologists called in (see the Historic Preservation Act on page 115) just to see if there was anything there. They found about 400 human remains, and after doing more testing and researching old maps and documents, they realized they had stumbled on the oldest African American cemetery in the country. The discovery caused many residents to rally for the site to be preserved, not built on. Thanks to the Historic Preservation Act and public outcry, this site is being developed into a memorial and museum to help preserve it.

Sites in Cities

◆ Historical archaeologists are interested in all kinds of events, including wars, battles, riots, shipwrecks, and even fires. Up until the early 20th century, fires were one of the most common disasters to occur in cities. The Fire of 1666 in London burned for five days and destroyed most of the city, including 13,000 homes and 89 churches. The Great Fire of Chicago in 1871 burned 17,000 buildings. An 1835 fire on a bit-

▲ *Fire can preserve artifacts such as coffee beans or fruits by carbonizing them. This scene shows an 1880 fire in New York City.*

terly cold December 16 in downtown New York City destroyed almost 700 buildings, and could be seen as far away as Philadelphia. As Philip Hone noted in his diary, "Goods and property of every description are found under the rubbish in enormous quantities." Archaeologists in New York have found the remains of food that was burned during the 1835 fire, including blueberries, coffee beans, peppercorns, grapes, and nutmeg located in the basement of Anthony Winans' grocery. Though you might think fire destroys everything in its path, in some cases, it can preserve the things it burns by removing the moisture from them and keeping them from being used or rotting away. When the moisture is gone, fruit can last much longer—think of raisins and prunes.

Many of the greatest historic finds are completely unintentional. Thanks to the U.S. Historic Preservation Act of 1966, any federally funded construction project has to begin with an archaeological test to see if there is anything of historic

Time Capsule

Time capsules have been used since the 1800s as a way of preserving the present so someone in the future can learn about what life was like. One of the largest time capsules in the world, 3,000 square meters, was sealed in a cave in California in 1966. In a way, all archaeological sites are time capsules, unintentionally left behind long ago.

MATERIALS
◆ *Several brown paper bags the size of small lunch bags*
◆ *5 personal items*
◆ *Pencil*
◆ *Pad of paper*

In this activity, you will learn to think like an archaeologist and try to learn something about your classmates. If you are not able to do this activity in school, get a few friends to do it with you. You will need five small items that you think would be good for a time capsule, and as many brown paper bags as you have friends or classmates. Include one for yourself. Place your items in your bag without letting others see what they are. Now write your initials on the bottom of the bag so you can get your stuff back later. Put all the bags in one place and take someone else's bag.

Empty the bag and look at the items. What are they? What can you tell your classmates about the person who owns them? How would you be able to tell what year the items are from? Is what your friend or classmate says about you based on your items true?

value at the site. Otherwise, once the construction begins, any archaeological artifacts might be damaged, destroyed, or buried for decades under pavement or a 70-story building. These days, many new buildings are skyscrapers, more than 20 stories high. The higher the building, the deeper the foundation has to be dug to keep the building from falling over; and the deeper the trench is dug, the more likely that artifacts will turn up from a previous century. As you read in Chapter 5, archaeologists in Frankfurt, Germany, found the remains of the ancient Roman settlement in the middle of the city.

Not all sites found in cities are accidental. When historical archaeologists know exactly where old buildings once stood, they can seize the chance when a building site is cleared to make room for a new skyscraper. This happened in New York when archaeologists uncovered the foundations of the Stadt Huys, the old Dutch City Hall from the mid-1600s. The stones were carefully recorded, numbered, and then reassembled in a display eight feet closer to ground level, so people passing by could see the discoveries.

Archaeologists in historic areas are often called in before a new road or building is built. The contractors (people who do the actual building) and owners have to stick to the environmental laws that say archaeologists should investigate to see if there is anything of significance at the site. If all that turns up are a few old nails and some broken bottles, construction can proceed. If archaeologists find a major site such as the African Burial Ground, construction can be delayed or even prevented. Sometimes, bulldozers and gasoline-powered augers (tools for boring holes in the ground) are used to get the job done more efficiently by scraping away layers of dirt and then taking a sample of earth deep into the ground.

The brilliant historical archaeologist James Deetz said, "It is extremely unlikely that any building constructed in the past has vanished

The remains of a 1600s Dutch tavern, found while digging foundations for a skyscraper, were raised closer to ground level and put in a display behind glass for people to see. ▼

without a trace." Archaeologists can find the site of an old house by discovering a few foundation stones, the remains of a cellar, a hearth, or even the remains of a few post holes. How is this possible? When wood decays, it leaves a darker, richer kind of soil than the surrounding dirt. Most soil is made of rock and organic material. Since all wood is organic, it will decay into a richer soil than ordinary dirt with lots of rock and sand. Digging carefully, archaeologists can find these remains and piece together where and how big the house was.

Historical archaeology is fun because it can be done wherever you live, unless you just moved

Historic Preservation

Historic preservation is the restoration and protection of old or historically significant buildings or grounds. Using old photographs, newspaper articles, and personal interviews with neighbors and elderly residents, buildings are brought back to their original appearance. By scraping off layers of paint—sometimes 10, 15, or even 20 of them—preservationists can see what the original colors were. Archaeology can be an important part of historic preservation, providing extra clues to what life was like and what kinds of everyday items people once used. As people around the world become more interested in their heritage, new preservation projects are started. Sometimes people also realize if they restore buildings or even whole neighborhoods, it will attract businesses and tourists. At the Long Pond Ironworks in Hewitt, New Jersey, abandoned and boarded-up buildings from the 1700s and 1800s sat gloomily along tree-lined Route 511 for many years, until a recent restoration. Now the grounds are open to the public, and there is a museum that highlights the history of the area, along with some archaeological artifacts found over the years.

Whole historic villages and towns can even be reconstructed from almost nothing using a combination of historic preservation and archaeology. The billionaire John D. Rockefeller funded the restoration of Colonial Williamsburg, Virginia, so archaeologists could excavate the sites of old buildings and use historic drawings, maps, and photos to reconstruct houses and shops from the 1600s and 1700s. Though most of the buildings in Colonial Williamsburg were heavily restored or are reproductions, many contain original artifacts that were dug up during ongoing excavations there. In Deerfield, Massachusetts, and Old Bethpage, New York, old wooden buildings were saved from certain destruction by being hauled in from other towns, sometimes dozens of miles away, to create a "new" historic village that looks similar to what an actual village might have looked like hundreds of years ago.

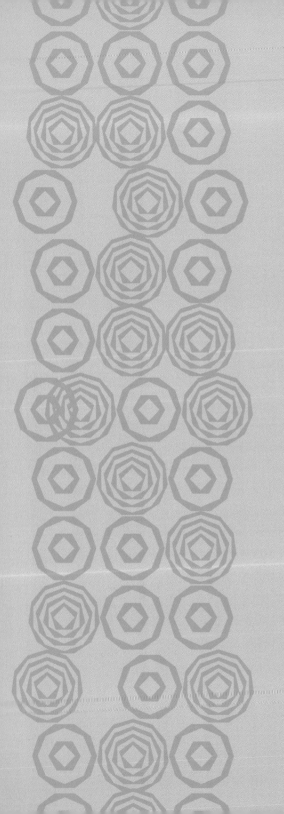

Dating Objects Using Patent Numbers

United States Utility Patents, or exclusive rights to the mechanical design or method of making an invention, were first given out in 1836. Many common items have a patent number on them, everything from hinges to hair dryers. Find some items in your home that have patent numbers printed or engraved on them and refer to the list below to see roughly when they were made. Usually, an item is within 10–20 years of its patent date because once the item is improved, a new patent number is issued. Sometimes there are several patents taken out on a particular invention; always go by the highest number listed.

Number 1	1836
Number 1,000	1838
Number 5,000	1847
Number 10,000	1854
Number 20,000	1858
Number 30,000	1860
Number 40,000	1863
Number 50,000	1865
Number 100,000	1870
Number 200,000	1878
Number 300,000	1884
Number 400,000	1889

Number 500,000	1893
Number 600,000	1898
Number 700,000	1902
Number 800,000	1905
Number 900,000	1908
Number 1,000,000	1911
Number 1,250,000	1917
Number 1,500,000	1924
Number 1,750,000	1930
Number 2,000,000	1935
Number 2,250,000	1942
Number 2,500,000	1950
Number 3,000,000	1961
Number 3,500,000	1970
Number 4,000,000	1976
Number 4,500,000	1985
Number 5,000,000	1991
Number 5,500,000	1996

A Design Patent is only for the design of an item, not the mechanical parts. The patent number has a "D" in front of it.

Number 1	1843
Number 1,000	1858
Number 2,000	1864

Number 5,000 1871

Number 10,000 1877

Number 20,000 1890

Number 30,000 1899

Number 40,000 1909

Number 50,000 1916

Number 60,000 1921

Number 70,000 1926

Number 80,000 1929

Number 90,000 1933

Number 100,000 1936

Number 125,000 1941

Number 150,000 1948

Number 175,000 1955

Number 200,000 1965

Number 225,000 1972

Number 250,000 1978

Number 275,000 1984

Number 300,000 1989

Number 350,000 1994

Number 400,000 1998

Look carefully at the lists. What seems to be happening to the number of patents issued as we go toward the present?

▲ *This artifact was found at an old dump. It says "Pat'd March 10, 1868." Patents were filed with the U.S. Patent Office and can be researched, so an archaeologist can look through the documents and find out how an item might have been used. The artifact in the picture is the top part of an old hand-held oil lamp.*

There is no limit to the kinds of documents that can help a historical archaeologist. For example, appraised lists (where each thing is valued by an appraiser, an expert in prices) of property from estates, invoices, bills, ledgers, and diary entries can tell you what kind of artifacts were being bought, sold, and used at the time and in the area you are excavating. The price or value of an item can tell you how rare and expensive it was compared to other things.

Look at the ledger entries from May 5, 1834, shown at the right. Can you find among the items listed a door, spikes, nails, glass, boards, and bricks? If this man bought bricks in 1834, and archaeologists find many bricks at the site of his house, it might be much easier to figure out where the bricks were made based on who sold them to him. Can you read the last name of the person who sold the bricks? Pick a room in your house or apartment and make an inventory of all the things larger than your hand. List how many of each item there are and include a brief description, for example, 1 large blue sofa, 1 small table lamp, 1 leather footstool, etc.

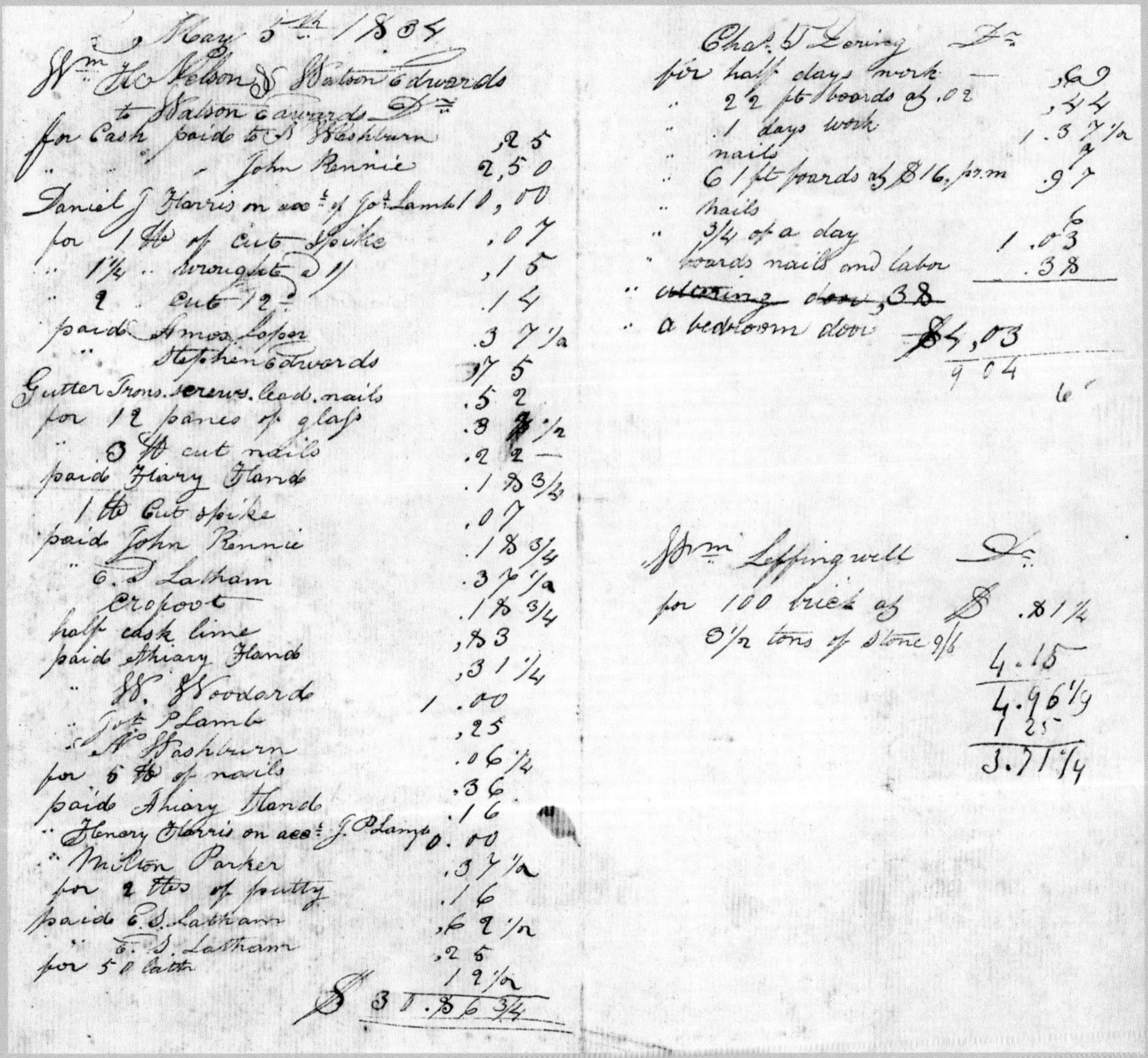
May 5th 1834
Wm H. Nelson & Watson Edwards
to Watson Edwards Dr
for Cash paid to N. Washburn .25
" " John Rennie 2,50
Daniel J. Harris on acct of Jos. Lamb 10,00
for 1 lb of Cut Spike .07
" 1 1/4 " wrought " .15
" 2 " Cut 12d .14
paid Amos Lopez .37 1/2
" Stephen Edwards .75
Gutter Irons. screws. lead. nails .52
for 12 panes of glass .87 1/2
" 3 lb cut nails .22
paid Hiary Hand .18 3/4
1 lb Cut spike .07
paid John Rennie .18 3/4
" C. S. Latham .37 1/2
Cropoot .18 3/4
half cask lime ,83
paid Ahiary Hand ,31 1/4
" W. Woodard 1.00
" Jos. P. Lamb ,25
" N. Washburn .06 1/4
for 6 lb of nails .36
paid Ahiary Hand .16
" Henry Harris on acct J. P. Lamb 10.00
" Milton Parker .37 1/2
for 2 lbs of putty .16
paid C. S. Latham ,62 1/2
" C. S. Latham ,25
for 50 lath 12 1/2
$ 31.86 3/4

Chas. T. Loring Dr
for half days work .69
" 2 1/2 ft boards at .02 ,44
" 1 days work 1.37 1/2
" nails .9
" 61 ft boards at $16. pr m .97
" nails .6
" 3/4 of a day 1.03
" boards nails and labor .38
" altering door .38
" a bedroom door $4,03
9.04
6

Wm Leffingwell Dr
for 100 brick at $ .81 1/2
8 1/2 tons of stone 9/6 4.15
4.96 1/2
1.25
3.71 1/4

into a brand-new house in a brand-new development—but even then, you never know! If you can get permission to dig in your backyard or some other nearby place, you might find old pieces of glass, bottle caps, nails, ceramics, or maybe even a coin or two. You can tell a lot by examining the items you find. What do the bottle caps say? Do the brand names still exist? What color is the glass? Is it curved or is it flat? Is it from a bottle or a window? Be careful to record exactly where you find each item and how deep in the ground it is, and wear canvas or leather work gloves so you don't cut yourself. Maybe your class can even organize a formal excavation project near your school. Just remember, the goal of historical archaeology is to use any and all available documents, maps, books, and magazines to help you understand the past even better.

Household Artifacts

◆ Once you have excavated a historic site, how can you date what you have found? You have already seen how dendrochronology works, but that cannot be used every time.

Archaeologists at historic sites have many ways of dating that archaeologists at prehistoric sites do not. Because excellent studio and factory records exist, ceramics, glassware, silverware, and even jewelry can be dated by type and pattern. Look in your china closet or kitchen cabinet. What does it say on the bottom of a dinner plate? Most china patterns were only made for a few years—even the most popular were only made for about 30 years, with slight changes that tell us if the china was made at the beginning or end of the 30-year period. And even a small fragment of china is dateable as long as part of the pattern is showing. Next time you visit your nearest large bookstore, see how many books you can find on dinnerware, china, and silverware patterns. Maybe you'll find a pattern that you have at home! Silversmiths in the 19th century and earlier had special marks they put on the bottom of their pieces called *hallmarks*. These could be any combination of initials, pictures, or symbols. There are books with hundreds of pages filled with these different hallmarks to identify when, where, and by whom the item was made.

If you take the oldest artifact that you find at a site, you know the site dates from no earlier than when that artifact was made. If a 1909 penny is the oldest artifact at a site, then the site had to be from 1909 or later. This kind of dating is called *terminus post quem*, from the Latin meaning "time after which." But imagine this scene—your family is planting a tree in your backyard, and while digging the hole, a nickel falls through a hole in your pocket and is eventually buried

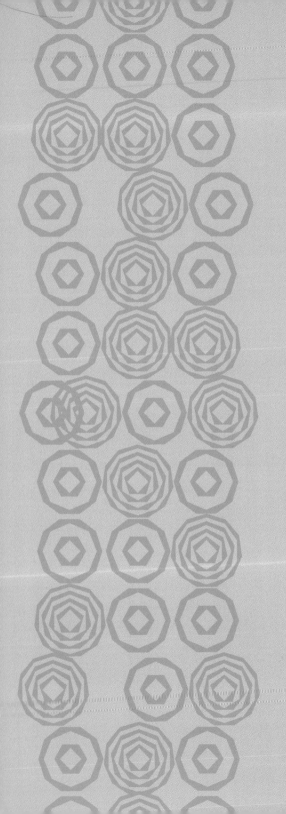

Genealogy is another tool historical archaeologists sometimes use to help them get a more complete picture of what life was like hundreds of years ago. By figuring out who lived in which house and what their occupations were, archaeologists can better understand the artifacts they find at the site. A farmer should have farming tools; a blacksmith, forging tools; a butcher, cutting tools and remains of animal bones.

Vital records like births, marriages, and deaths, and census records can give archaeologists an idea of how the population of a town changed over time, including which people lived where and for how long, what their occupations were, what their nationalities were, and what diseases they died from. In many towns around the world, you can find buildings that are 200, 300, and even 400 years old still standing. In those cases, the ground nearby is less likely to have been disturbed. These places might be good candidates for archaeological digs. Matching artifacts to people's names and lives is extremely helpful in getting a more complete picture of what life was like. Most vital records are available through local libraries, your local archives, or the National Archives, which has branches all over the country. Many vital records are now available on the Internet.

MATERIALS
◆ *Pencil or pen*
◆ *2 sheets of paper*
◆ *Calculator*

Looking at early city directories or telephone books can tell you a lot about a place. The kind of occupations people had is a direct reflection of the technology of the time and the customs and businesses of the people who lived there. In Dutch New York, for example, taverns made up $\frac{1}{4}$ of all businesses. Archaeologists can figure out which neighborhoods were mostly shops, which ones were mostly manufacturing, etc.

On your sheets of paper, make the following headings, leaving several lines between each: Food, Clothing, Liquor/Bar, Janitor/Cleaner, Clerk, Shopkeeper, Furniture maker, Artist/Actor/Musician, and Miscellaneous. Now look at the page shown here from an 1899 city directory. Starting with Edward Vogler and ending with Philip Volkel, write down each person's occupation under the appropriate heading and put a single line next to it. The second time you come across the same occupation, add a second line on your paper next to that occupation.

Now count the total number of lines you have drawn, representing the total number of people you have counted. Divide the subtotal for each category of business, such as Food, by the total. Multiply that number by 100 to get the percentage of all occupations dealing with that category. This is just a sampling, meaning it is just a small portion of the available data. Even fairly small data samples can give an accurate projection of what the complete data would show. That is why polls used to predict presidential elections reflect only 1,000 people out of the millions who will actually vote.

Which type of businesses or occupations are the most popular in your sample? Which are the least popular? How do you think these numbers would be different in today's world?

Vogler Edwd manager 1730 Bway
—Elizabeth wid Chas h 83 3d
—Geo h 526 E 152d
—Geo liquors 216 W 84th
—Hy brewer h 201 E 93d
—Jacob P clerk h 423 W 49th
—John butcher h 869 2d av
—John G dressgds 362 Bway h Pa
—Julius publisher 5 E 14th h Undercliff N J
—Lawrence carpenter h 621 E 138th
—Louis finisher h 561 E 154th
—Nicholas police h 526 E 152d
—Peter cigars 341 E 10th
—Wm porter h 533 W 52d
Vogrich Max composer h 105 Madison av
Vogt Adam packer h 1590 1st av
—Albert ins 25 Malden la h 133 Eldert Bklyn
—Amelia h 819 E 145th
—Anton janitor h 2077 8th av
—Anton jeweler 25 Malden la h 1807 Bklyn av Bklyn
—Arnold bartender h 842 Trinity av
—Arthur G tobacco 164 Front h 279 Hart Bklyn
—Arthur H ins 29 Liberty h 99 Henry Bklyn
—August metalgds 169 Wooster h 2138 S Boulevard
—August pres 206 E 86th h 324 E 82d
—Bertha wid Peter h 503 E 118th
—Carl lawyer h 212 W 105th
—Chas agent h 212 W 105th
—Chas butcher h 438 W 52d
—Chas engraver 194 William h 101 Nostrand av Bklyn
—Chas jr tobacco 164 Front h 825 Bwick av Bklyn
—Chas E printer h 212 W 105th
—Chas F barber 201½ E 62d h 253 E 62d
—Chas H dyer h 746 Columbus av
—Christian J engraver 194 William h 16 Stockton Bklyn
—Dora grocer 335 7th av h 162 W 29th
—Edwd awningmkr h 506 W 46th
—Frances wid John h 651 Prospect av
—Frank H tobacco 164 Front h 268 Hart Bklyn
—Fred baker h 131 Av C
—Fred polisher h 648 10th av
—Fred sweep 236 Sullivan
—Fred wagons 474 Water
—Fred A liquors 100 W 3d h 95 W 3d
—Geo carpenter h 690 9th av
—Geo liquors 477 Gwich h 500 Canal
—Geo meat 377 Hudson
—Geo tailor h 180 Av B
—Geo tailor 305 E 85th
—Geo J roofer 1124 3d av h 320 E 66th
—Geo P tailor h 381 E 10th
—Gustav engraver 194 William h 101 Nostrand av Bklyn
—Gustave toolmkr h 674 E 163d
—Hy liquors 312 W 39th
—Hy manager h 415 E 58th
—Hy printer h r 151 1st av
—Hy A drugs 1691 Lex av h 151 E 106th
—Hy F real estate 228 E 36th
—Herman butcher h 517 2d av
—Jacob manager 406 W 53d h 404 W 53d
—Jacob varnisher h 500 E 14th

—John J stable 539 Lex av & express 57 W 16th h 107 W 17th
—Wm J stable 539 Lex av & express 57 W 16th h 107 W 17th
Vogue (periodical) 3 W 29th
Vohl August waters 159 Elizabeth h 12 Spring
—Jacob tailor 558 3th av
—Philip cabinetmkr h 213 W 124th
—& Co waters 159 Elizabeth
Vuhlantt Carl musician h r 407 E 15th
Vohmann John candy 1687 Av A
Vohmann Carl cotton 19 Whitehall h Stapleton B R
Vohrallk Jos carver h 438 E 77th
Vohrer Danl machinist h 522 E 88th
—Hy clerk h 248 W 31st
—John janitor h 315 W 26th
Vohringer Christopher cabinetmkr h 81 E 4th
—Louis carpenter h 607 E 9th
—Theodore printer h 609 E 9th
Voice of Missions (periodical) 61 Bible h
Voight Wm fireman h 502 E 56th
Voigt Adolph birds 131 Division
—Albert clerk h 304 E 83d
—Alfd H salve 242 Canal h 48 Lee av Bklyn
—August smith 161 9th av
—Carl E correspondent h 1044 Prospect av
—Chas F preserves 315 E 75th h 448 E 78th
—Cornelius trucks 500 E 148th
—Edwd C packer h 306 W 68th
—Frank tailor h 435 E 17th
—Fred printer 1334 2d av
—Geo J smith Grant av VanNest pk
—Geo Wm pickles 442 E 78th
—Gustav eatingh 18 St Marks pl
—Gustav painter 709 Elton av h 577 E 158th
—Gustav jr painter 709 Elton av h 577 E 158th
—Gustave electrician h 148 8th av
—Hy safemkr h 601 E 150th
—Hy E F printer 242 Canal h 48 Lee av Bklyn
—Hy W salve 242 Canal h 48 Lee av Bklyn
—Jacob radish 315 E 75th h 448 E 78th
—John coal 464 Robbins av
—John G & Son salve 242 Canal
—Jos shoes 315 E 70th
—Louis F clerk h 354 E 17th
—Max modeler h 518 E 84th
—Max G milk 323 E 9th
—Moritz smith 161 9th av
—Oscar milk 431 E 12th
—Rudolph packer h 408 E 9th
—Rudolph paints 385 Amsterdam av h 503 Amsterdam av
—Theresa wid Oscar bdgh 16 3d
—Wm grocer 613 Amsterdam av h 151 W 90th
—Wm machinist h 248 E 121st
—Wm painter 214 E 108th h 119 E 108th
—Wm tailor 125 5th av
—Wm A cutlery 67 Reade h Boonton N J
—Wm F preserves 452 E 78th
—M & Son smiths 161 9th av
—Bros plaster 242 Canal
—& Son painters 709 Elton av
—, Starr & Co cutlery 67 Reade
Voigtlaender & Son Optical Co 467 W 14th
Voigtlander Walter musician h 535 E 87th
Voigts Herman J agent h 117 E 116th
Voiland Chas bronzewkr h 406 E 23d

169 E 73d
—Geo V hardware 36 W 3d h 169 E 73d
—C L & Co hardware 36 W 3d
Volckmann Chas manager h 240 E 33d
—Nicholas h Kossuth av Wakefield
Volckmer Hy bookbinder 204 Church h 212 45th Bklyn
—& Zimmermann bookbinders 204 Church
Vold Constant flowers h 76 W 3d
Volence Vincent grocer 1577 1st av h 1365 1st av
Volenti Lawrence barber 301 E 45th h 304 E 45th
Volgenau Chas A candy 2402 Amsterdam av
—Hedwig A wid Adolph variety 2163 Amsterdam av
Volger Bernard G pads 32 Vesey h 270 Decatur Bklyn
—Wm B pads 32 Vesey h 464 Central pk W
—W B & B G pads 32 Vesey
Volgin Aaron mer 85 Canal h 134 E 113th
Volgmann Fred H janitor h 312 W 116th
Volini Michl drygds 18 Prince h 25 Prince
Volnino Dominick coal 613 Columbus av h 771 Columbus av
Vollno Geo pedlar h 66 Thompson
—Peter tailor 84 Spring h 78 Spring
—Pietro shoes 5 Prince h 60 E 4th
—& Sica tailors 84 Spring
Volinsky Julius tailor 323 3d h 1590 Madison av
Volk Adam shoes 2127 2d av
—Albert smith h 723 Washn
—Chas F eatingh 76 & 84 Church h Terrace pl n Eagle av
—Eberhard liquors 661 8th av & 209 6th av h 151 W 16th
—Emil engraver 78 Nassau
—Frances wid Chas grocer 1336 Stebbins av
—Frank electrician h 187 E 4th
—Fred h 304 E 34th
—Fred clerk h 551 W 159th
—Fred electrician h 231 Alex av
—Fred embds 1156 3d av
—Geo E tailor h 286 E 10th
—Geo W cashier 119 Bway h Bklyn
—Harris pedlar h 226 Madison
—Hat Co 29 Washn pl
—Hy h 733 Elton av
—Jacob L boxmkr h 301 E 76th
—John carpenter h 450 E 88th
—John publisher 28 State h 181 51st Bklyn
—John shoer 503 Water h 77 Montgomery
—Jos florist 1451 2d av
—Jos A sec 29 Washn pl h 8 Norwalk Ct
—Louis butcher h 214 Madison
—Mary wid Hieronymus h 422 W 49th
—Peter shoes 313 E 8th
—Sussman provns 86½ Delancey h 118 Orchard
—W Douglas sec 215 W 57th
—Wm eatingh 1742 2d av
—Wm liquors 209 6th av & 661 8th av h 663 8th av
—Wm painter h 1273 1st av
—Bros liquors 209 6th av & 661 8th av
Volkamer Jos shoes 1383 3d av
Volke Adolph engineer h 326 E 31st
—Mary nurse 326 E 31st
Volkel Chas carpenter h 676 E 152d
—Emil R furs 436 6th av h 25 Mhtn av
—Madeline wid Geo h 709 E 9th
—Philip butcher h 556 W 38th

Archaeologists at historic sites are always concerned with who owned the property and for how long. Their excavations at the remains of an old house might reveal many personal items, such as bottles, pipes, buttons, jewelry, pots, plates, and silverware. As you saw earlier, knowing what people's occupations were and where they lived is very useful to archaeologists. When archaeologists excavate in rural places, they don't have city directories to help them figure out when people lived in certain houses. The federal census is only useful for estimating because it is taken every ten years.

One of the best documents for a historical archaeologist in a rural area is the property deed. This document is a certificate of ownership for a piece of land. It describes the land, where it is, who is selling it, who is buying it, and for what price. Because names of roads may have changed over time, natural features such as creeks or rivers can help identify where a parcel of land described hundred of years ago is located.

Look at the deed from the year 1857. How much land was sold? What was the price? Do you think it would be easy or difficult to find this piece of land today? If your parents own a house, ask them to show you the deed. How does it differ from the 1857 deed? It should still tell you how much land they own and from whom they bought it. It might even say when the house was built.

beneath the tree. Many years later, archaeologists come in to dig at the site. They find all kinds of artifacts dating to the early 20th century, but they also find the nickel that says 2000 on it. This may confuse archaeologists, but if everything else at that level of the ground seems to be 90 years older, they will probably assume that there was some kind of tampering with the soil that occurred during, or shortly after, the year 2000.

Sometimes, archaeologists working at prehistoric sites find ancient arrowheads and shell remnants mixed in with broken glass and iron nails. They know this mixing happened because modern people interfere with the ground a lot more than ancient people did. Modern people dig wells, cesspools, and foundations for buildings; and they also take dirt from one place and bring it to another to build roads and highways, make artificial lakes and ponds, and plant trees whose roots can interfere with the stratigraphy of sites. In these cases, the Law of Superposition that Heinrich Schliemann used when digging at Troy does not apply.

There is still another method of dating that is even harder to use, because there are very few times when it will work successfully. This dating method is called *terminus ante quem*, meaning "time before which." If you were digging in downtown New York City, and you hit the still-preserved burnt layer of earth from the Great Fire of 1835, you would know that anything below that layer had to be from the "time before which" the fire occurred, in other words, before 1835. However, if you were digging and you found not a complete layer but small patches of charred remains, you would know there was some interference since 1835 and you could not say for sure if what was below was from before 1835 or not.

Now that you know more about historical archaeology, find out when the city or town you live in was first settled. Is there a historic society or museum? Have there been any excavations in your town? Find out if anything once stood on the piece of land where you now live. You might be surprised to discover that prehistoric peoples thousands of years ago, such as Native Americans, lived on the very same land as you.

That is why archaeology is so fascinating—because we all share this planet, not only with each other, but with our ancestors and distant relatives. They may be long gone, but the bits and pieces of their lives that archaeologists piece together make certain their stories live on forever.

Glossary

Aerial photography—taking pictures from hundreds or thousands of feet above ground level to reveal archaeological features or patterns in the ground.

agriculture—the intentional growing, harvesting, and storing of crops on a large scale to feed many people at once.

antechamber—a room whose main purpose is to serve as a hall or entry into a larger, more elaborate room.

archaeologist—someone who studies and excavates (removes from the ground) the remains of past cultures.

artifact—anything archaeologists find that has been modified by humans for their use.

association—two or more artifacts found together that have a relationship to each other.

Australopithecus—apelike creature that lived about 4 million years ago and had some human characteristics.

Aztec—Mexican civilization that was destroyed by invading Spanish in 1519.

Bering Strait—body of water between Alaska and Asia that was once land, allowing the first human settlers to cross over to the Americas.

Carbon 14—a method of dating organic artifacts by measuring how much of the radioactive element carbon 14 is left.

Carnarvon, Lord—the English noble who sponsored Carter's excavations in Egypt.

Carter, Howard—the English archaeologist who discovered Tutankhamun's tomb in 1922.

chopper—a stone tool used for chopping and crushing.

civilization—a group whose people live in cities, have a system of writing or record keeping, rely on agriculture, and control a large territory.

conservation—the cleaning and preservation of artifacts once they are removed from the ground.

context—the place and situation in which an artifact is found.

core—the part of a stone that is left when smaller pieces are chipped away.

cuneiform—the wedge-shaped writing system of the ancient Sumerians.

Decompose—break apart into tiny pieces that become part of the soil.

dendrochronology—a method of dating archaeological sites by using tree rings.

domestication—the taming and breeding of animals, either as pets or for food.

Ecofact—anything an archaeologist finds that is an animal or plant remain that was partly eaten or used by humans, but not modified for use as a tool or decoration.

excavation—careful measuring, recording, and digging into the ground to look for archaeological remains from the past.

Feature—a very large, hard-to-remove artifact, such as a wall or a well.

flake—a piece of rock that falls off when a larger rock is chipped.

Glaciers—huge masses of ice that exist only in the coldest parts of the world.

Great Pyramid—largest of the Egyptian pyramids, built for the king named Cheops (also known as Khufu).

Hand ax—one of the earliest tools, it was a stone with an edge that was used to cut.

historical archaeologist—an archaeologist who focuses on the period of time after about 1500, when historical records and documents start to exist.

Homo habilis—the "handy man" who lived in Africa beginning more than 2.5 million years ago and made the first stone tools.

Homo heidelbergensis—the creature similar to *Homo erectus* that spread through Europe.

Homo erectus—the "upright man" who lived in Africa beginning nearly 2 million years ago.

Homo ergaster—the creature similar to *Homo erectus* that spread through Asia.

Homo sapiens neanderthalensis—advanced humanlike creature that developed flake tools, and coexisted for a short time with modern humans.

Homo sapiens sapiens—the scientific name for modern human beings.

Ice Age—period when glaciers advanced southward and covered much of the Northern Hemisphere.

Inca—a Peruvian civilization that ended abruptly when the Spanish conquered them in the early 16th century.

inventory—a list of household items, usually made to settle an estate of someone who has died.

Lascaux—the cave in France where magnificent prehistoric paintings were found in 1940.

Layard, Austen—Englishman who excavated in Mesopotamia during the 19th century and sent many large statues and walls back to the British Museum.

Mastaba—an early, flatter precursor to the Egyptian pyramid.

matrix—the dirt or other material surrounding an artifact in the ground.

Maya—a Central American civilization that peaked in power between A.D. 250 and A.D. 900.

megalith—a large stone transported and/or carved/decorated by ancient people.

Mesolithic—the "middle stone age" (beginning about 12,000 B.C.), when agriculture and experiments with sedentary (living in one place) lifestyle began.

microlith—a tiny stone tool with a special function.

Munsell—color chart used by archaeologist to describe soil colors.

Neolithic—the "new stone age" (beginning about 6000 B.C.), when technological innovations, agriculture, and domestication of animals were commonplace.

Organic—anything that is or was once alive (plant or animal).

Petrie, Sir Flinders—archaeologist who studied Egypt and helped popularize seriation as a method of dating.

Pompeii—a Roman town that was buried by the eruption of Mount Vesuvius in A.D. 79.

potassium argon—method of dating volcanic rocks that are found near human remains or artifacts.

Radioactive—an element that is unstable and subject to decay over long periods of time.

Schliemann, Heinrich—German archaeologist who discovered the ancient city of Troy.

seriation—dating artifacts by putting them into a series relative to each other, from oldest to newest.

Shang Dynasty—the first civilization in China.

stelae—large stone sculptures found at Mayan sites in Central America.

stratigraphy—the layering of earth, showing different colors and types of soil.

superposition—a general rule about layers of earth, stating that the oldest layers are at the bottom and the most recent layers are at the top.

sympathetic magic—ancient religious belief that if you draw something, it will happen.

Tundra—low to the ground, unassuming plant life that grows in extreme cold.

Ur—one of the most important Sumerian cities, excavated by Wooley beginning in 1922.

View—a detailed drawing from above of a town or city, showing all the houses and streets. These were common between the 1500s and the 1800s.

Wooley, Sir Leonard—an English archaeologist who excavated Sumerian sites, including the Royal Cemetery at Ur.

Web Sites for Further Exploration

Jamestown Rediscovery Web Site

www.apva.org/jr.html

The Association for the Preservation of Virginia Antiquities site explains the history of Jamestown and recent archaeological discoveries.

The Leakey Foundation

www.leakeyfoundation.org

Read news stories about the famous Leakey family's recent fossil discoveries, or gather information about the Leakey Foundation's work.

About.com's Archaeology Site

archaeology.miningco.com/science/archaeology

This is a great site for finding articles on many archaeological subjects, including a list of current archaeological excavations around the world.

United States Patent and Trademark Office

www.uspto.gov/patft

Look up information on patents and view patent old applications at the United States Patent and Trademark Office's online site.

Discovering Archaeology

www.discoveringarchaeology.com

This magazine site features many stories about current finds and archaeological mysteries.

Archaeology

www.archaeology.org/main.html

Archaeology magazine's site features stories about recent archaeological discoveries.

Dig

dig.archaeology.org

Visit the online site of *Dig* magazine, a publication especially for kids.

University of Pennsylvania

www.upenn.edu/museum/collections/
    ourexhibits.html

The University of Pennsylvania's museum site features online archaeological exhibits.

Society for Historical Archaeology

www.sha.org

Find out more about a career in historical archaeology.

Egypt Revealed

www.egyptrevealed.com

Current stories about Egyptian archaeology and mysteries can be found at this magazine's site.

Kid Arch

www.binghamton.edu/cap/kidindex.html

This site is especially geared toward teaching kids about archaeology.

The American Memory Site

memory.loc.gov

The U.S. Library of Congress's American Memory site features documents and maps relating to the history of the United States, including presidential papers.

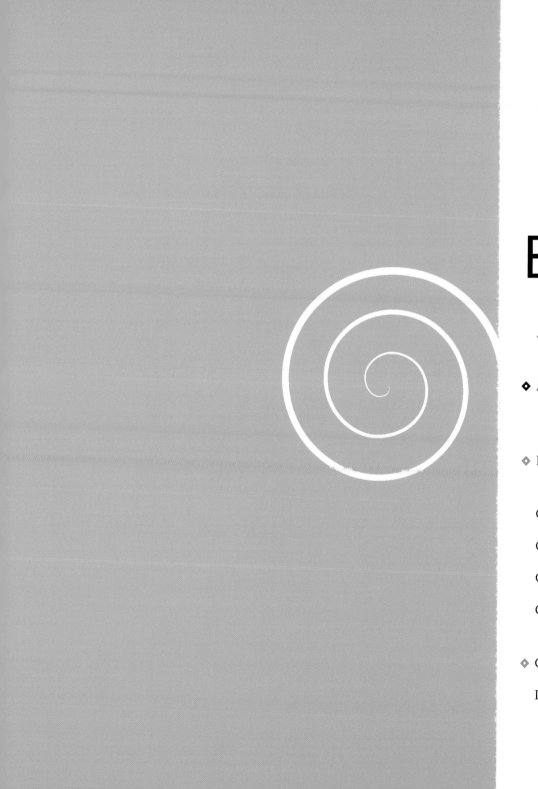

Bibliography

Andrews, Roy Chapman. *Meet Your Ancestors: A Biography of Primitive Man.* New York: Viking Press, 1963.

◆ Ashmore, Wendy, and Robert J. Sharer. *Discovering Our Past: A Brief Introduction to Archaeology.* Mountain View, CA: Mayfield Publishing Co., 1988.

◆ Broida, Marian. *Ancient Egyptians and Their Neighbors.* Chicago: Chicago Review Press, 1999.

Caulfield, Max. *Ireland.* New York: Barnes & Noble Books, 1993.

Ceram, C. W. *Gods, Graves & Scholars.* New York: Vintage Books, 1986.

Collier, John. *Indians of the Americas.* New York: Mentor Books, 1947.

Constable, Nick, and Karen Farrington. *Ireland.* New York: Barnes & Noble Books, 1997.

◆ Corbishley, Mike. *Secret Cities.* New York: Lodestar Books, 1989.

Daniels, Steve, and Nicholas David. *The Archaeology Workbook.* Philadelphia: University of Pennsylvania Press, 1982.

Deetz, James. *In Small Things Forgotten: The Archaeology of Early American Life.* Garden City, NY: Anchor Press/Doubleday, 1977.

Feder, Kenneth L. *Frauds, Myths, and Mysteries: Science and Pseudoscience in Archaeology.* Mountain View, CA: Mayfield Publishing Co., 1990.

◆ Gilbert, Katharine Stoddert, ed. *Treasures of Tutankhamun.* New York: Ballantine Books, 1976.

Horvath, Miklos. *Aquincum.* Budapest: Budapest Historical Museum, no date.

Kohn, David. "A Golden Find: An Untouched Burial Site Entices Egyptologists." *Newsday.* New York: January 11, 2000, pp. C8–C9.

Lamberg-Karlovsky, C. C., and Jeremy A. Sabloff. *Ancient Civilizations: The Near East and Mesoamerica.* Prospect Heights, IL: Waveland Press, Inc., 1979.

Lyman, Susan Elizabeth. *The Story of New York.* New York: Crown Publishers Inc., 1964.

◆ MacDonald, Fiona. *The Traveler's Guide to Ancient Greece.* New York: Scholastic, 1998.

◆ Martin, Ana. *Prehistoric Stone Monuments.* Chicago: Children's Press, 1991.

Marx, Robert F., and Jennifer Marx. *The Search for Sunken Treasure.* Toronto: Key Porter Books, 1993.

◆ McKeever, Susan. *Ancient Rome.* New York: Dorling Kindersley, 1995.

Muzej, Narodni. *Lepenski Vir.* Belgrade: National Museum, 1979.

◆ Nicholson, Robert, and Claire Watts. *The Vikings.* New York: Scholastic Inc. 1991.

Patrick, Richard. *All Color Book of Greek Mythology.* London: Octopus Books Ltd., 1972.

Reece, Richard. *Identifying Roman Coins: A Practical Guide to the Identification of Site Finds in Britain.* London: Seaby, 1986.

Silberman, Neil Asher. *Digging for God and Country: Exploration, Archaeology, and the Secret Struggle for the Holy Land, 1799–1917.* New York: Anchor Books/Doubleday, 1982.

Sklenar, Karel. *Hunters of the Stone Age.* London: Heineman Publishers, 1988.

Smith, William. *A Smaller Dictionary of Greek and Roman Antiquities.* London: John Murray, 1860

◆ Stiebing, William H., Jr. *Uncovering the Past: A History of Archaeology*. New York: Oxford University Press, 1993.

◆ Terzi, Marinella. *The Chinese Empire*. Chicago: Children's Press, 1990.

◆ Whalen, Frank D., Wallace West, and Claudia West. *New York Yesterday*. New York: Noble and Noble, 1949.

◆ Wyler, Rose, and Gerald Ames. *The Story of the Ice Age*. New York: Scholastic Book Services, 1956.

◇◇◇◇◇◇◇◇◇◇◇◇◇◇◇◇◇◇◇◇◇◇◇◇

◆ books more suitable to a younger audience

◆ an excellent adult-level book that gives a good history of how archaeology developed

Photo Credits

p. 6 *courtesy of Donald Proulx*

p. 8 *courtesy of Donald Proulx*

p. 9 *courtesy of Donald Proulx*

p. 10 *photo by author, courtesy of John Vetter*

p. 13 *photo by author, courtesy of Garvies Point Museum, Glen Cove, NY*

p. 24 *photo (right) by author, courtesy of Garvies Point Museum, Glen Cove, NY*

p. 35 *courtesy of Kathleen Freedman*

p. 37 *photo by author, courtesy of Garvies Point Museum, Glen Cove, NY*

p. 43 *courtesy of Robert Panchyk*

p. 44 *courtesy of Caren Prommersberger*

p. 51 *courtesy of Caren Prommersberger*

p. 53, B *courtesy of Eva Arvai*

p. 53, D *courtesy of Jean Prommersberger*

p. 53, F *courtesy of Eva Arvai*

p. 65 *(both) courtesy of Kathleen Freedman*

p. 69 *courtesy of Amy Newman*

p. 72 *courtesy of Kathleen Freedman*

p. 77 *courtesy of Amy Newman*

p. 88 *photo by Richard Panchyk, courtesy of National Museum of the American Indian, Smithsonian Institution (10/5860)*

p. 89 *(both) courtesy of Donald Proulx*

p. 91 *courtesy of Amy Newman*

p. 94 *courtesy of Donald Proulx*

p. 97 *courtesy of Katherine Panchyk*

p. 98 *courtesy of Katherine Panchyk*

All other photos by the author or from the author's collection. All prints from the author's collection.

Index

Page numbers shown in italics denote photographs or illustrations.

A

D

Danube River, 41
Dart, Raymond, 16
dating, methods of, 11–12, 33, 121
   carbon dating, 33
   denrdochronology, 111
   hallmarks, 121
   Law of Superposition, 125
   patent numbers, 118–119
   potassium-argon dating, 33
   seriation, 52
   terminus ante quem, 125
   terminus post quem, 121
   tree rings. *See*
      dendrochronology
Dawson, Charles, 21-22
Dawson's Dawn Man, 22
decompose, 18
Deerfield. *See* Massachusetts
Deetz, James, 116
Delaware, 108
Delphi, *77*
dendrochronology, 111
Denon, Dominique, 49
density, 7
Description of Egypt, 49
dinosaurs, 15
Diocletian, 82
divers, 73

domestication, 39–40
Dubois, Eugene, 21
Dutch, 102, *103*, 108, 116, *116*

E

earthquakes, 19, 96
ecofacts, 93
Egypt, 1–3, 49-50, 63, 68, 76, 82
   Alexandria, 3, 63
   Bahariya, 50
   Pyramid, Djoser's, 49
   Pyramid of Cheops, 48
   pyramids, 47–50, *48*
   Valley of Kings, 2, 56
Egyptians, 48, 52, 54
electrical current, 6
England, 3, *4*, 12, 22, *43*, 54, 55, 81, 86, 111. *See also* Britain
   London, 55
   Piltdown Common, 22
   Stonehenge, 43, *43*
Eoanthropus dawsoni, 22
Erech, 57
erosion, 19
Ethiopia, 16
ethnographers, 16
Euphrates River, 54, 56, 82
Euripides, 76

Europe, *6*, 21, 23, 30, 34, 36–37, 81, 88, 91, 95, 104, 106
excavation, 5, 8–13, 16, 55, 88–89, 91, 97

F

farming, 37, 39, 41, 45
feature, 11, 93
Fertile Crescent, 54
fire, 71, *114*, 114–115, 125
flint, 20, 22
Florida, 108
Fountain of Siloam, *81*
France, 37, 50, 81, 86, *106*
   Lascaux, 34
   Normandy, 86
   Paris, 50, *106*
Frankfurt. *See* Germany
Fredericksburg. *See* Virginia
French, 59, 108

G

Gama, da, 108
Garvies Point Museum. *See* New York
genealogy, 122
genus, 20